Youth and Social Class

Alan France • Steven Roberts

Youth and Social Class

Enduring Inequality in the United Kingdom, Australia and New Zealand

Alan France
School of Social Sciences
University of Auckland
Auckland, New Zealand

Steven Roberts
Monash University
Clayton, Victoria, Australia

ISBN 978-1-137-57828-0   ISBN 978-1-137-57829-7 (eBook)
DOI 10.1057/978-1-137-57829-7

Library of Congress Control Number: 2017938572

© The Editor(s) (if applicable) and The Author(s) 2017
The author(s) has/have asserted their right(s) to be identified as the author(s) of this work in accordance with the Copyright, Designs and Patents Act 1988.
This work is subject to copyright. All rights are solely and exclusively licensed by the Publisher, whether the whole or part of the material is concerned, specifically the rights of translation, reprinting, reuse of illustrations, recitation, broadcasting, reproduction on microfilms or in any other physical way, and transmission or information storage and retrieval, electronic adaptation, computer software, or by similar or dissimilar methodology now known or hereafter developed.
The use of general descriptive names, registered names, trademarks, service marks, etc. in this publication does not imply, even in the absence of a specific statement, that such names are exempt from the relevant protective laws and regulations and therefore free for general use.
The publisher, the authors and the editors are safe to assume that the advice and information in this book are believed to be true and accurate at the date of publication. Neither the publisher nor the authors or the editors give a warranty, express or implied, with respect to the material contained herein or for any errors or omissions that may have been made. The publisher remains neutral with regard to jurisdictional claims in published maps and institutional affiliations.

Cover pattern © Harvey Loake

Printed on acid-free paper

This Palgrave Macmillan imprint is published by Springer Nature
The registered company is Macmillan Publishers Ltd.
The registered company address is: The Campus, 4 Crinan Street, London, N1 9XW, United Kingdom

For the Jan in each of our lives

Acknowledgements

We would like to thank Anna Bull and Garth Stahl for their insightful and helpful comments on our penultimate draft. While the final analysis is ours their contributions was invaluable. We would also like to thank Amelia Derkatsch and Sharla Plant our editors at Palgrave for their support and to Harriet Barker, who in commissioning us to write this text, created the opportunity for it to come to life. Special thanks (as always) need to go to the two Jans who continually keep our feet on the ground!

Contents

1 Introduction 1

2 Class Matters 9

3 Education, Social Mobility and the Enduring Nature of Class 39

4 Young People, Work and Social Class 69

5 Youth, Class and Intersectionality 101

6 Conclusion: Towards a New Agenda for Youth Sociology 135

Index 143

CHAPTER 1

Introduction

Abstract Despite class analysis enjoying a recent revival in mainstream sociology, influential claims that 'class is dead' or class is a 'zombie category' have had a longer standing impact on youth sociology. Such claims have proven instrumental in minimising class analysis in understanding the lives of young people in the UK, Australia and New Zealand, with recent and rapid social change being used as the basis for arguing class does not offer the tools to explain the choices and decisions of the young. We disagree, and in this book we draw on the work of – and those influenced by – Pierre Bourdieu to show that class is not only relevant but should also be a central and key component of analyses of young people's experiences.

Keywords Sociology · Class · Youth · Pierre Bourdieu · Social reproduction

> Spanning the generations, a plain fact of this matter is that only a minority of young people have been able to decide what/who they wish to become well in advance, then implement their aims. This kind of active individualisation is class based. (Roberts 2003: 23–24)

Youth sociology is often a field of investigation where core sociological concepts are contested and debated. Advances and debates in sociology do, however, sometimes have limited impact in this field and this, we suggest, is especially relevant to the question of social class. This is not to say that social class has not been discussed or theorised in youth sociology – on the contrary, as we shall show by presenting a historical backdrop, youth sociology in many ways emerged out of a core interest in class. That said, the influence and position of social class in the field of youth sociology has waned and in fact almost disappeared in more recent times. Such developments appear to question the certainty imbued in the position outlined earlier in the quote from Ken Roberts. Therefore, our central contention in this book is twofold. First, we want to show how recent theorisations on the production and experience of inequality in a period of rapid social change have served to (often inadvertently) marginalise the significance of social class in our thinking. Secondly, by drawing on Pierre Bourdieu's scholarship and more recent works that have critically and constructively built on his ideas[1] we plan to show that such developments cannot only be contested and challenged but also used to illuminate how social class is being socially reproduced for the young in changing times.

It is also worth recognising at this point what this book is not aiming to do and what we are not claiming. First, we are not in the business of creating new ways of categorising and measuring class in late modern society. We, along with others[2] want to steer away from such a task, drawing instead on Bourdieu's suggestion that we must recognise '...what exists is not "social classes" as understood in the realist, substantialist and empiricist mode of thinking...but rather a *social space* in the true sense of the term [that is]...reciprocal externality of the objects it encloses' (Bourdieu 1987: 3). As such, by drawing on a wide range of recent international evidence, we intend to show how social class is socially reproduced and lived, by the young, across and through social space. This is not to deny differences between groups or classes only that we need to concentrate on identifying how some groups maximise their opportunities and socially reproduce and maintain class difference. We expand on this point in the discussion that follows in Chapter 2. Secondly, we are not claiming that our analysis is complete. In fact, like others working in this area[3] we see this book making a contribution to the debate on the relevance and role of social class, especially for the young in late modern times. We believe that much conceptual and empirical work is still required to take our analysis further. Our approach is to 'put class back on the map' in youth sociology and to show how and why it should remain not just variably present but central to the analysis of young people's lives, even in periods of rapid social change.

Our approach is one that considers that a '...Bourdieusian sociology of class possesses the means to make sense of not only the current nexus of domination but its genesis too' (Atkinson et al. 2012: 4). Building on and blending insights from writings such as Fiona Devine and colleagues' *Rethinking Class* (2005), Will Atkinson's *Class Individualisation and Late modernity* (2010), Beverley Skeggs' *Formations of Class and Gender* (1997) and *Bourdieu: The Next Generation* by Thatcher and colleagues (2016), this book will present an understanding of the relationship between the continuity of classed relations and the changing nature of the expression of such inequalities. Our aim, then, is to argue that youth sociology does and can do much more than outline the ways class remains as integral for predicting origins and destinations, and instead reveal the ways that class is a dynamic of history, a lived experience and something which is in continual production and allows us to better understand the process of exclusion and broader inequalities. Ultimately, while some have argued that measures of the differential progression of groups against institutional markers provide little understanding of how difference is produced and how greater equality may be achieved, the book will argue that this can be done by foregrounding social class in the way that we set out.

Complementing our Bourdieusian approach, we will use a variety of international evidence from the UK, Australia and New Zealand to illustrate how his tools are useful in this process. Much is made of the 'Britishness' of class theory, suggesting that it has limited traction in other national contexts and we want to show that class can and does operate across national boundaries. Australia and New Zealand have been selected as examples outside of the British context and have been chosen partly for personal reasons. We are both British-born but now reside and work over in the antipodes and we are continually frustrated by positions taken in these countries, both politically and academically, that continually deny the value of class analysis in explaining young people's life trajectories.

As we have said, our focus in making class 'visible' is to bring together a wide range of theoretical and empirical projects that illuminate and highlight how class is being reconfigured in late modernity and how social reproduction is maintained and operationalised. We do, however, need to recognise that in the antipodes there has been less theoretical and empirical work on class than in places like the UK. For example, measures of class in Australia and New Zealand are usually replaced with Social and Economic Status (SES) measures. The lack of engagement with this as a possible 'class' measurement in official but also academic pieces across the antipodes seem to either ignore class or deny its importance, something we try to show is fundamentally problematic. The theorising of class in the antipodes has also been limited and the work of Bourdieu (especially around class questions) has not made major inroads on sociology in the antipodes. These developments have consequences for our analysis in that there is not always the empirical or theoretical work going on that helps in such a task. Where possible we have tried to draw on work that is illustrative of his approach or evidence that re-enforces class differences, but we also recognise there remain 'gaps' to be filled. One of the key purposes of this book is to try to reinvigorate this debate and to show how the work of Bourdieu might prove useful for youth researchers working on class-related issues in highlighting the salience of class in these changing times in the antipodes, as well as the UK. Our approach to doing this, given some of the gaps and differences we set out here and in more detail in later chapters, is to avoid 'case study' approaches for each country in favour of a more blended discussion, highlighting differences and similarities between the three countries and their related respective research findings as we proceed.

Following this introduction, Chapter 2 starts by briefly sketching out the history of class, showing its centrality, in Britain. We will also illuminate how class operates in Australia and New Zealand; even though it is usually rhetorically denied or ignored we want to show that it still matters. We will also show how youth sociology has historically studied the question of class. In this, we will set out the problematic treatment of class in more contemporary discussions. Advocates of approaches focusing on diverse issues such as 'political economy' and 'post subcultures' are challenged for their limited focus and conceptualisation of how class operates across the 'cultural' domains. Here, we will also trace the ways in which the potential dilution of social class emerging in such accounts (to a greater or lesser extent) has implications for a wider diminishing and nigh on abandonment of the language of social class in political discourses. The chapter's other purpose is to present the key building block in the book's narrative; the salience of Bourdieusian readings of social class as essential to the contemporary study of youth and young people's 'lived experience'. We contend that adopting Bourdieu's theoretical resources more fully allows us to reconfigure, sometimes reject and often plug some of the conceptual gaps that proponents of newer theories put forth.

The next two chapters are each dedicated to demonstrating how class matters and is being socially reproduced in a particular aspect of young people's lives. Our focus here is primarily on 16–24 year olds and in particular on their movements through education, training and work. This is not to deny that class inequality and social (im)mobility have a strong connection to compulsory schooling (see Ball 2008) only to suggest that in more recent times we know very little about how these processes operate once the young leave schooling. As we show in the introductions to each chapter, major social and political changes have been taking place across the UK, Australia and New Zealand that have reconfigured the 'school-to-work transition' and by drawing on a wide range of sociological studies we show how the work of Bourdieu and Bourdieusian scholars are helping to illuminate the processes of class social reproduction.

In the final chapter, we turn our attention to the relationship that social class has with other inequalities. Class theory (including that of Bourdieu) has been criticised for its failure to understand the impact of other inequalities on young people's lives. We show in this chapter how a Bourdieusian approach to class can help us not only understand other inequalities but also grasp their interrelationship with class. To achieve this, we focus on the areas of gender and race and the recent theorising around the concept of intersectionality. Again, we want to suggest that youth sociology has given little attention to the work on intersectionality and that a way forward for making sense of the relationship between class, gender and/or race is to develop a more sophisticated reading of this process. To illustrate this, we draw upon innovative work in gender and race studies that use a Bourdieusian approach and also combine their analysis with class. We do, however, suggest that 'more needs to be done' to show a deeper understanding of this relationship. In the final section of this chapter, we turn our attention specifically to the lack of theorising of social class in Australia and New Zealand around the question of the indigenous populations. Again, theorising and empirical evidence is thin on the ground but we suggest ways that a Bourdieusian approach could help bring this issue to the foreground in looking at the situation of New Zealand Māori and Aboriginal and Torres Strait Islander young people in Australia.

Correspondingly, and across all chapters, we try where possible to show not only how class operates in young people's lives but also how it impacts on their independence, their interdependency, their social geographical mobility and their use of space and place. All of these are dimensions that inflect the numerous social, economic and cultural realities of young people's lives. For example, on the theme of interdependence, the erosion of young people's ability to access the housing market, alongside the growing debt and uncertainty about secure and well-paid work has increasingly delayed the achievement of economic and housing independence (France 2016). This in turn redoubles the importance of family relationships to young people's life chances and demonstrates how going from youth to adulthood is 'inextricably bound up' (Scott 2005: 2) with the lives of others, particularly family members. In such a context, classed inequalities experienced by parents as well as by young people can often become compounded.

Notes

1. See Thatcher et al. (2016), for example.
2. See Atkinson (2015), for example, for a good discussion on this matter.
3. See Savage et al. (2013, 2015).

References

Atkinson, W. (2010). The myth of the reflexive worker: Class and work histories in neo-liberal times. *Work, Employment and Society*, 24(3), 413–429.
Atkinson, W. (2015). *Class.* Cambridge: Polity Press.
Atkinson, W., Roberts, S. & Savage, M. (Ed.). (2012). *Class inequality in Austerity Britain: Power, difference and suffering.* London: Palgrave Macmillan.
Ball, S. J. (2008). *The education debate: Policy and politics in the twenty-first century.* Bristol: Policy Press.
Bourdieu, P. (1987). What makes a social class? *Berkeley Journal of Sociology*, 32, 1–17.
Devine, F., Savage, Scott, J. & Crompton, R. (2005). *Rethinking class: Culture, identities and lifestyle.* London: Palgrave MacMillan.
France, A. (2016). *Understanding youth in the global economic crisis.* Bristol: Policy Press.
Roberts, K. (2003). Problems and Priorities for the Sociology of Youth. In A. Bennett, S. Cieslik, and S. Miles (Eds.), *Researching Youth.* Basingstoke: Palgrave MacMillan.
Savage, M., Devine, F., Cunningham, N., Taylor, M., Yaojun, L., Hjellbrekke, J., Le Roux, B., Friedman, S., & Miles, A. (2013). A new model of social class? Findings from the BBC's Great British class survey experiment. *Sociology*, 47(2), 219–250.

Savage, M. (2015). *Social class in the 21st century*. London: Pelican.
Scott, J. (2005). *Teenagers at Risk: A Prospective Study of How Some Youth Beat the Odds to Overcome Family Disadvantage*: ESRC Research Summary, http://www.researchcatalogue.esrc.ac.uk/grants/L134251027/outputs/read/660614bb-bdc3-4a27-9441-83965cb26620.
Skeggs, B. (1997). *Formations of class and Gender: becoming respectable*. London: Sage.
Thatcher, J., Ingram, N., Burke, C., & Abrahams, J. (Ed.). (2016). *Bourdieu: The next generation*. London: Routledge.

CHAPTER 2

Class Matters

Abstract Although class theory is gaining resurgence in British sociology, it has been for many years marginal to much sociological theorising and its impact on other countries such as Australia and New Zealand has been limited. While youth sociology historically emerged out of concerns about working-class youth it has, since the late 1990s, become substantially marginalised, either seen as irrelevant or having less significance for understanding young people's lives. This chapter sets out to explain why this has been the case and to challenge this perspective by proposing that the work of Pierre Bourdieu can help illuminate how class is operating in contemporary times.

Keywords Class theory · Youth sociology · Antipodes · Pierre Bourdieu

CLASS: A VERY BRITISH PHENOMENA?

A motivation for this book has been a desire to challenge the idea that class only really operates in the UK and/or the Northern hemisphere. As we will show in the following, while class in the antipodes has had a chequered and diverse history, in the imagination of both the public and the academic literature, when brought under the microscope it can be observed as a very powerful force that structures and shapes the lives of young people in the antipodes. This process of illumination, we believe, is greatly aided by the work of Pierre Bourdieu because his theoretical tools can help us make class more visible – a point we return to towards the end of this chapter.

Of course, it is well recognised that class is a very British invention. Works of historians such as E.P. Thompson (1963) and Eric Hobsbawm (1968) squarely located the emergence of the British class system within the shift from Feudal society to Industrial society and the emergence of the capitalist modes of production in the period of enlightenment. Capitalism was a very powerful force, creating a distinctive working and upper class system that shaped the distribution of wealth and incomes and opportunities. Across time, class has then been recognised as a core feature of British society. Not only did it influence the creation of political parties (i.e. the Labour party being for the working classes and the Conservatives for the upper classes), but it also created and reflected distinctive geographical differentiation across the UK, with strong suggestions that the place one lived was a strong indication of social class.

As a part of this process of recognition of class, the British government also created a sophisticated classification system that measured a person's class position. Despite these early developments, more recently British governments and various academic studies[1] have, one after another for several decades, continually claimed class to be less influential, that social mobility for the working class is possible, and/or actively refrained from using the word 'class' in political and policy discussion. Such claims have been continually challenged (Goldthorpe 1980; Savage 2015; Atkinson 2010), yet any lack of social mobility remains situated in political rhetoric as a problem of the individual; this is partly a driver for us writing this book. While we recognise what class looks like has changed over time, it can and does continue to matter in the lives and choices of British young people.

The social class to which an individual 'belongs' has major consequences not only for future 'destinations' but also for how they are perceived and received in British society. Being working class is often framed as an individual's own fault, choice or failing and therefore is closely bound with perceptions of the working class as 'scroungers', 'lazy' or an 'underclass' that is 'undeserving'. Recent analysis of the 'chavs' stereotype provides a case in point. As is made clear by Owen Jones's (2011) *Chavs: The Demonization of the Working Class* and Imogen Tyler's (2013) *Revolting Subjects*, these processes of blame and demonisation are still very much at work, with fashion choices and other behaviours of the young working class being constructed as tasteless and worthy of the title 'scum'.

Beyond such analyses, class has been back more fundamentally in the public imagination in the UK. First, the great British Class Survey (Savage et al. 2013) was launched, which drew upon Bourdieu's concepts as a way of measuring class in contemporary times. The results showed a seven-tier system, highlighting class was still very much alive in the UK,[2] with a most significant contribution being to illuminate how the elite class operate to maintain their position of advantage, even in times of austerity (Savage 2015). Secondly, in relation to the British electorate's decision to exit the European Union, clear evidence emerges that the 'leave vote' was driven by a disaffected and disillusioned 'working class' in areas of high deprivation who saw an opportunity to have their voice heard (Swales 2016). So, what we observe is not only is Britain accredited with being the creator of class society, but also that class is strongly recognised in the public imagination as an essential feature.

Class in the Antipodes

While Australia and New Zealand are somewhat similar 'liberal states' to the UK, they have very different histories that have produced differently organised societies. For example, while both are former colonies of the British Empire, Australia is a Federal State that locates much power in large regional governments, while New Zealand has the Treaty of Waitangi that defines the relationship between Māori, its indigenous population, and the state. Class in these two countries, in many cases, is denied, rejected or thought out of step as a concept, but it does operate less visibly, 'behind the scenes' so to speak, and is a powerful determinant of life chances.

We should start by recognising that the idea of New Zealand and Australia being class-based societies has not held in the public imagination. In fact, as many of us working in the antipodes will be aware, it is often casually claimed that Australia and New Zealand, unlike the UK, cannot be understood through a class lens. Simon During noted in 1998 that in its formation New Zealand constructed itself as a nation that embraced traditional British values of 'hard work' and nationhood with clear allegiances to the 'mother country', while also claiming uniqueness in '... its absence of class difference, its affluence and equality, its affable, sincere sociability, its untroubled "race relations"'(During 1998: 34). This is no better symbolised than through the sport of rugby. In England, rugby emerged and has been fundamentally run as an upper-middle class game, with strong links to public schooling,[3] whereas in New Zealand, rugby was positioned as 'a symbol of mateship, intrepidness, coloniser-colonised reconciliation' (During 1998: 35). Its inclusiveness of Māori and others of lower SES backgrounds helps underpin claims that New Zealand's national identity is classless and egalitarian (Falcous and McLeod 2012). In a sense, these ideas were embedded in 'New Zealand thinking' early into the colonising process in that early settlers wanted to build a land-owning nation that supported and encouraged social mobility (Wilkes 2004). As the country matured, it became seen as a 'social laboratory' with progressive policies towards equality. It is therefore no coincidence that it was the first nation to give votes to women, to introduce pensions and the first economy to create a welfare state based on Keynesian economics. New Zealand saw itself as a forward thinking, inclusive nation.

From the post-war period onwards, New Zealand actively set about the process of 'nation building', trying hard to create a more inclusive society. Radical movements, such as anti-nuclear movement that created New Zealand as a nuclear free zone and the anti-apartheid movement that campaigned for the banning of the South African rugby team playing in New Zealand, were important to this process. Alongside this, however, was growing recognition that New Zealand was a racially divided nation and, after a number of major national protests and campaigns,[4] the Treaty of Waitangi[5] tribunal was set up to address historical injustices of colonialism (Carlyon and Morrow 2013). As a result, the nation-building project of subsequent governments became overtly concerned with race relations, but said very little on class divisions. Unlike in the UK, the instruments constructed by governments for measuring social strata were not defined by *social class* classifications but by a related *but different* notion of Social and Economic Status[6] (which included employment status, income and education). From the 1980s, the key political question was not about tackling inequality between the classes, per se, but how to encourage greater social mobility of Māori and Pacific peoples, denying in many cases that race and class were closely intertwined.

Australia followed its own trajectory, but is also seen as a classless society in the public imagination. While Australia started as a penal colony with a regimental status and hierarchy of a 'total institution', it did not last for long and the 'national character' that emerged was one that admired the 'underdog' and had a '...foundation of loyalty, respect, and fairness between individuals' (Greig et al. 2003: 167–168). Stemming from the egalitarian ideal of 'mateship' – an (albeit masculinist) communal social conscience that promoted solidarity in response to hardships experienced by early penal migrants, then, later, soldiers in the First World War – notions of 'fairness' and 'equity' came to pervade everyday language. The country's legal framework established in the 'national character' the notion that Australia was an 'egalitarian' society that rejects class as a social division: the land of the 'fair go', where all could enjoy the possibility of doing well, was inscribed into the public imagination. In 1996 the then Prime Minister Howard said that Australians should be proud of '. . . having built one of the most prosperous, most egalitarian and fairest societies in the world' (Howard 1996 quote in Greig et al: 168). Similar to New Zealand, the Australian government does not measure social class, using instead the same measures of SES, refusing to categorise people into social class groups. So, what we see in both Australia and New Zealand are perspectives that embed into the psyche of the nation a view that they are 'progressive meritocracies' where class and other 'social divisions' had been avoided, a view that, while unsubstantiated, today remains influential shaping public discourses of class inequality.

Dispelling the Myth of 'Classlessness' in the Antipodes

Even during the arrival of initial Western colonisers, a perspective of New Zealand and Australia as classless seemed to ignore the reality of colonialism. Thrupp (2001), indeed, suggests that in New Zealand's emerging economy of early colonialism employment seemed to mainly be self-employment and trades, making it difficult to see class stratification; yet, a 'new class' was being established. With the expansion of urban centres and the stealing and selling of Māori land, a class structure was created that saw Pākehā[7] landowners take possession of large farming areas, while Māori and other more English working-class settlers were employed as either domestic workers, farm labourers or workers in small industries in urban centres. By 1852 over 78% of those employed in Auckland were working in low-skilled professions and manual work (Wilkes 2004). Australia's class structure was also quickly established in the labour market after the first phases of colonialism. As urbanisation and international trade escalated and Australia entered into capitalist world markets, a more complex division of labour took hold that saw a new urban working class develop alongside a local, mercantile capital class (Connell and Irving 1980). Such developments grew in influence as Australia became an international exporter. Of significance is that one of the key practices exported by the British Empire was the creation of a professional class of civil servants who were employed in government to manage the new colonies. This helped establish a new middle class in both Australia and New Zealand, contributing to the expansion of not only a class structure but also an ascendant middle class that was both white and male (Wilkes 2004).

More importantly, in contemporary times, when we examine the distribution of wealth and income in New Zealand and Australia we see significant inequalities exist between social groups. If we think of classes being formed by the '...mechanisms of accumulation...' that have the '...potential to augment, store, transmit, and convert advantages' (Savage et al. 2015) then the levels of inequality in countries have much to tell us about class. For example in New Zealand,[8] in terms of income the bottom 30% earn less than NZ$15,000, the bottom 50% earn less than NZ$24,000 and 70% of the total population earn less than NZ$43,000. At the top of the earnings ladder the top 5% earn a minimum of $93,000; the top 2% earn over $131,000; the top 1% earn over $170,000, while the top 0.4% earn over $250,000. In terms of wealth ownership a similar pattern exists. In total, the 2.9 million adults in New Zealand own almost NZ$470 billion. The top 1% alone own 16% of the total wealth (approximately NZ$77billion – amongst 29,000 adults). The top 10% owns just over 50% of all wealth, while the bottom 50% of New Zealand adults (1.45 million adults) own just 5% of wealth. In fact, New Zealand's top 1% owns three times as much as is owned collectively by the bottom 50% of the population (Rashbrooke 2013).

A similar picture exists in Australia. The average income of households in the top 20% is five times the income of households in the bottom 20%. At the extremes of the distribution, the average weekly after tax income of the top 5% is 13 times that of the bottom 5%. The average income of a household in the top 10% of the income distribution is AUS$4,189, while average income in the bottom 10% is AUS$496 a week after tax. Within the top 10%, income is highly concentrated.

> Since 1978, 75% of the increase in income of the top 10% has gone to the top 1%, and 65% has gone to the top 0.1%. In 2012, average income for the 180,000 individuals in the top 1% was $400,000 per annum (per person not household) while the minimum income of a person in the top 1% was $211,000. There are also 18,000 people in the top 0.1%, with an average income of $600,000. (Australian Council of Social Service 2015: 17)

Wealth ownership in Australia is more unequally distributed than income. For example, a person in the top 20% has around 70 times more wealth than a person in the bottom 20%, while the top 10% of households own 45% of all wealth, most of the remainder of wealth is owned by the next 50% of households. Similar to New Zealand the bottom 40% of households own just 5% of all wealth. Wealth ownership in Australia has also been increasing with the average wealth of a person in the top 20% increasing by 28% over the past 8 years, while for the bottom 20% it increased by only 3% (Australian Council of Social Services 2015). So, what we see in New Zealand and Australia is a continued set of economic divisions that cannot be simply read as a difference between the poor and the rich. A recent study in Australia (Sheppard and Biddle 2015) attempted to link these divisions to class. Drawing on Savage et al.' (2013) UK-based study,[9] they discovered five observable classes in Australia described as established affluent, emergent affluent, mobile middle class and established working class. These divisions we constructed around the share of economic, social and cultural capital. Similar to the UK study, it illuminated the extent of the affluent class and its continuing influence in Australian society.

However, while the language of class is missing from Australia and New Zealand, this does not mean class is necessarily invisible. Sheppard and Biddle, (2015: 2) suggest that 'Social Class is a little like "swagger" it is hard to define, and tough to measure but you know it when you see it'; i.e. Australians know class when they see it. This is perhaps most evident around the distinction between bogans and hipsters. As Threadgold suggests, these two social groups '...have become quintessential floating signifiers of young (and not so young) people participating in an array of consumer cultures. They enable distinction to be performed and ascribed while eschewing the very notion of class.'[10] Hipsters tends to be equated with being middle class, while the bogan is perceived as a feared and ridiculed working-class 'folk devil'. It is not unusual for the concept to be linked to the notion of 'chav' in the UK (Pini et al. 2012), with both positioned and presumed uncouth, racist, masculine, aggressive, uneducated and having bad dress sense. They are usually both seen as a term of abuse for the white working poor. One of the most recent developments is that bogans have been seen to benefit from the recent boom in Australia (unlike their British counterparts). These 'Cashed Up bogans' have then been further vilified and attacked by the middle classes as

'...superficial, fraudulent and tasteless...' with the aim of distancing themselves and reassuring their power and position as moral leaders (Pini et al. 2012: 152).

While such language is not so pervasive in New Zealand, a recent newspaper article on the appointment of Paula Bennett as Deputy Prime Minister described her as a 'bogan' because she comes from a working class back ground and was a solo mum.[11] New Zealand also shows signs of other particular classed processes that rarely are named as such, for example engagement with the international extended working holiday phenomenon, 'the overseas experience' (OE). The OE is discursively positioned as a national ritual, or a symbol of adulthood, and at the same time as a choice that a young person makes in New Zealand's presumed egalitarian society. Yet, despite the colloquial understanding of the OE as something that 'everyone does', research finds that it tends to be an exclusionary practice (Haverig and Roberts 2011). The OE is predominantly taken up by middle-class young people, those who go to university rather than taking vocational tracks through education, and only open to those with adequate economic and cultural resources (Haverig and Roberts 2011). Even then, rather than indicating some form of freedom, there seems to be underlying classed process at work that make the OE a 'compulsory freedom', a practice of distinction required to indicate one is a middle-class New Zealander.

Theorising Class

So what has been happening in respect of the *theorising* of class in sociology? Class theory in sociology has a long and illustrious history; it could be argued that class is the most dominant feature of sociological theorising across time and space. Class analysis was, of course, emerged from the classic work of Karl Marx and continued through the writings of Max Weber and Emile Durkheim. These theorists shaped our understanding of how classes might be formed and how they impacted social life. More contemporaneously, class theorising, especially in the Northern hemisphere, has been driven by debates within and between American and British sociologists and has been dogged by questions of measurement and classification (Atkinson 2015).

Throughout the 1960s and until the late 1990s, class theory was shaped by 'analytical Marxism', most notably by E.O. Wright (1978), and also by Goldthorpe's (1980) 'neo-Weberian' approach. Yet, these two approaches also had a number of major problems that distanced sociologists from class-based analysis. First, they had little to say about the 'lived experience' of class or 'what "class" actually means to people or how it affects how people relate to and judge one another on a daily basis' (Atkinson 2015: 60). Secondly, by locating its analysis within occupational structures it failed to understand the interrelationship both *within* classes and with other forms of inequality (Devine et al. 2005). Thirdly, all the studies on occupation struggled to explain and understand 'class-consciousness' and how people positioned themselves in the class structure (Devine et al. 2005). Finally, there was a failure to understand the actions of the wealthy. Classes were seen as being linked to occupation and therefore little was said about how those who owned wealth (either by the transference of assets or by accumulation of wealth through investment) operated. The work of Goldthorpe and others concentrated on the relationships between the working and middle class and on the boundary between the middle and working class and as a result it has brought about '... a preoccupation with what might be seen as "liminal" classes, standing at the threshold of the fundamental collar divide' (Savage 2015: 226).[12]

As the relevance of class theorising in sociology has been challenged internally to sociology, others within utopian traditions and cultural studies also argued that class was becoming less relevant in people's lives. Gorz (1982), for example argued in his book, *Farewell to the Working Class*, that the shift from an industrial to service and information society saw a new set of relations emerge that changed the structure and relevance of the working class. These arguments gained further ground in a similar debate emerging in the 1990s, where Pakulski and Waters (1996) argued that 'class was dead'. They proposed that the concept of class was too crude and incapable of handling the newly emerging 'identity politics'. They suggested class was a historical phenomenon that had become a theoretical 'straightjacket', holding little relevance in contemporary times. The 'class is dead' theme was furthered by debates in sociology that were strongly influenced by post-modernism and post-structuralism.

One of the major writers in this tradition was Ulrich Beck (1992). He argued that the new logic of societies was about how to manage risks, such as global warming, nuclear disaster and food contamination, and that consequently class (both its advantages and disadvantages) is less significant to how it is to be managed. Moreover, he claimed that the 'risk society' has given rise to a wide range of new interest groups and movements that emerge less from 'class struggles' and more from uniting victims (or potential victims) of risk. He suggests we have seen the

'... demolition of the large-group categories of industrial society as the fonts of identities, life situations and inequalities' (Atkinson 2010: 18). In its place, he suggests, was the emergence of individualisation, where people are disembedded from social forms such as class and are being 're-embedded' in new ways where they must 'cobble together their biographies' (Beck 1997: 95). Beck goes on to argue that in this context 'class' as an analytical tool becomes a 'zombie category'; obsolete and unhelpful in helping us understand individual lives (Beck-Gernsheim 2002: 201–13).

This attack on class theory was furthered by Bauman (2001), who argued that late (or what he calls 'liquid') modernity is now characterised by the process of 'disembedding' without re-embedding. Giddens similarly followed in being 'anti-class', although he takes a more Weberian approach in suggesting that as globalisation has expanded (and accelerated) the self has increasingly become a 'reflexive project' (Giddens 1991: 5) with new *lifestyles* needing to be created in the place of tradition, collective culture and action, and a corresponding need to life-plan with '... the general thrust of his argument being: neither self-identity nor social action are tethered any longer to class positions' (Atkinson 2010: 28).

The positions held by Beck, Bauman and Giddens generated substantial engagement, especially from the Goldthorpe (Goldthorpe 2002, 2007; Goldthorpe and McKnight 2006). Along with others (Skeggs 2004; Brannen and Nilsen 2005; Fevre 2007), they argued that Beck, Bauman and Giddens each created a 'data free' form of grand theory that remained detached from the empirical world and reality. This data free theorising was criticised for uncritically becoming a part of a public discourse that reinforces the idea that class has limited relevance in the 'new' order being created by capitalism (Atkinson 2010). Not only this, Goldthorpe is highly critical of the limited literature that the proponents of the new order use to make their arguments. For example, when a more thorough review of literature is undertaken in issues such as life chances, educational attainment and social mobility class clearly seems to be significant in shaping outcomes for both the poor and the wealthy (Goldthorpe and McKnight 2006; Roberts 2010).

CLASS THEORY IN THE ANTIPODES

Similar to the UK, class theorising in Australia and New Zealand has become marginalised. Much of the early sociology in Australia was focussed on 'scientificity' that saw sociological investigation being

'...pure, replicable description...' (Connell 2015: 357). A core task for sociology, therefore, was about explaining and identifying what constitutes Australian society. It was highly critical of 'abstract empiricism' and argued for a strong methodological focus on social surveys as a way of identifying trends and patterns. As Connell (2015) suggests, sociology in Australia was greatly influenced by the idea that it was part of the modernisation project, which then gave justification for comparisons with USA, UK and Canada as these were other modern industrial democratic societies. This of course had a major influence in the direction that theorising of class took hold in Australia (Connell 2015). Woodward and Emmison (2009) suggested that the history of class theorising in Australia can be divided into three strands. First, stratification research oriented in a Marxist tradition (Connell and Irving 1980); secondly, a quantitative tradition that drew upon large social surveys and statistical methodologies (Graetz and Mcallister 1988) and finally an approach that was strongly influenced by the work of Erick Olin Wright and also that of the neo-Weberian sociologist John Goldthorpe (Baxter et al. 1991). But by the end of the 1990s, Australia's interest in class waned and the 'class is dead debate' dominated discussions about the relevance of class theorising in sociology (Martin and Wajcman 2004). The ideas of Pakulski and Waters (1996) took hold, creating scepticism over its relevance for explaining social change in Australia. The response from those advocating for class to be central to any analysis concentrated on '...arid exercises in statistically based semantics...' (Martin and Wajcman 2004: 180), and the literature on class failed to explore causes or group strategies that maximised opportunities and advantage over others. It seemed unable to find a way of understanding class in changing times. As we will see in the following, the 'class is dead thesis' in Australia then gained momentum within youth sociology through the work of social generational theorists who advocate that social change is making class a redundant 'zombie' category (Woodman 2009).

New Zealand has a similar history, although its marginalising of class studies took a slightly different route. Throughout the 1970s and into the 1990s a number of studies, influenced by British and American sociology of the labour market, attempted to show that class held relevance in New Zealand. Pitts (1977), for example, brought together a collection of essays from New Zealand Marxist sociologists that argued for a recognition of class and its relationship to the means of production. Others followed suit, drawing on both Marxist and neo-Weberian approaches. One such piece was a major study led by Wilkes (1985), who attempted to construct a class-based analysis by drawing E.O. Wright's measures. Yet, by the 1990s, class studies seemed to have again lost flavour with sociologists. With the coming of neoliberalism and 'Rogernomics',[13] interest in class as a subject to be studied declined. Roper (1997), for example, was critical of the failure of social science in New Zealand to recognise how the class structure was becoming reshaped. He reasserted the importance of recognising that the classed nature of New Zealand society was not only being maintained but also increased (Roper 1997). Crothers suggests that the decline of studies of class is partly a result of New Zealand governments having an '...ambivalent relationship with measures of inequality and class' (Crothers 2013: 259) but also that

> biculturalism and identity politics emerged in the 1970s and was then more generally put on the political agenda by Rogernomics as its area of 'social conscience' this locked-in these issues for consideration at the expense of adequate attention to Class/Inequality as an issue (Crothers 2013: 273)

By the early 2000s, then, class theorising had become marginal to mainstream sociology. With the growth of post-modernism and identity politics, the shift away from class theory was significant. That said, a school of work, especially within the UK, set about driving a new approach to understanding class drawing on the ideas of Pierre Bourdieu (Devine et al. 2005). Much of the work was a rejection of the 'cultural turn' in sociology and the influence of post-modernism, but there was also a strong desire to maintain class analysis within the sociology of education (Ball 2002; Walkerdine et al. 2001). From this we have seen a growth of class studies emerge and expand. Atkinson (2009, 2010, 2015), for example, has set about reasserting the value and importance of class theorising, while Savage et al. (2013) created new measures of class in the UK. In the northern hemisphere, then, class is somewhat re-emerging, especially as a body of evidence is starting to empirically support the theoretical claims of Bourdieusian scholars – a point we will expand in the following.

The Importance of Youth and Class

As outlined in Chapter 1, our attention to class analysis stems from our own interests in youth sociology. While much mainstream theorising about class ignores youth, seeing young people as not having a class identity of their own, we are interested in this group because this is where class identities and futures are continually socially reproduced and established.

Youth sociology has a long held interest in class and especially social reproduction. This is borne out in the ways that class was for long periods an essential cornerstone in youth-focussed research and theorising, but equally in how its relevance has been debated, especially in the last 30 years, or even absent or attacked with varying degrees of hostility. Here, we draw attention to the way that the significance of class also came under attack from within the field.

Until the late 1990s youth sociology closely associated itself with class theorising. For example, after the immediate post-war period it was, in some quarters, heralded as a golden period, where young people's transitions to adulthood were thought to be smooth and relatively unproblematic,[14] and wider society experienced, as we note before, the process of 'embourgeoisement'. However, just as Lockwood, Goldthorpe and colleagues challenged the assumption that economic development had considerably transformed working-class lives, youth scholars also sought to demonstrate that class and status relationships were, at least in part, independent from changes in the economic, technological and ecological infrastructure; that is, class difference remained a stubborn feature of life. This was depicted in multiple accounts in what are often known as the two 'traditions' youth research: the 'transition tradition' and the 'cultural tradition'. The former school of thought looked to understand the structuring role of social class in respect of young people's experiences of and pathways through education and the associated later life-chances in terms of employment outcomes. This has been a perennial question for studies following what is often described as the 'transitions' approach to studying youth. Two excellent contributions to this area come from Carter (1966) and Ashton and Field (1976). Both illustrated the incongruence between working-class young people's expectation and realities of the youth labour market, and especially the impact of social class background on school-to-work transitions. Class was clearly on the map and located in relationships with the labour market.

On the other hand, the 'cultural' tradition of youth studies also took up the challenge of critically exploring the notion that youth was a relatively homogenously experienced life-course phase. This is most commonly associated with research conducted by critical sociologists at the University of Birmingham's Centre for Contemporary Cultural Studies (CCCS) in the 1970s, who applied social class as a centrally significant issue in their analysis of what they described as youth 'subcultures'. Paul Willis's (1977) research into working-class boys' resistance to education is a classic in this field of work. Retaining the CCCS class-focussed lens, but supplanting the notion of subculture with the idea of counter culture, Willis's analysis leaned towards subject matter (i.e. school and work) that was of interest to those looking at transitions to (now famously) implicate working-class boys as complicit in the process of social reproduction that ensured working-class kids get working-class jobs – their recognition of the 'objective limits' of the labour market and the relevance of schooling for the lives that lay ahead being a central to this. While this received criticism for its focus on boys (Griffin 1985; McRobbie 1978), it showed how class was being socially reproduced.

Class analysis came to characterise the transitions branch of youth research, and a considerable evidence base was developed (e.g. Ashton et al. 1990; Roberts 1995). Empiricism was key, with the CCCS project positioned as lacking in suitable data to make the claims that it had made (Blackman 2005). That said throughout the 1990s a wide range of cultural studies also continued the CCCS tradition of exploring the process of social reproduction in the labour market (e.g. Finn 1987; Hollands 1990: Bates and Riseborough 1993; Mizen 1995). These all highlighted in a variety of empirical studies how the 'new' training state operationalised social reproduction of young people into working-class careers and futures. Similar developments took place in Australia. While some of the early work was concerned with statistical modelling of school-to-work transitions (Connell 1983), various studies explored how class and culture, particularly in schools and training, contributed to social reproduction of class (Connell 1983; Dwyer et al. 1984). This was not necessarily echoed in New Zealand, though.

The sociology of youth, of course, was far from immune to sociology's wider cultural turn and the 'death of class' claims. Indeed, the broader sociological currents asserting the need to move beyond structural determinism (e.g. Nash 2001) were echoed very strongly by some youth sociologists who were keen to contribute to a 'switch of [sociological] focus from institutional and structural features of society to the study of culture' (Wolff 1999: 501). This shift from more structural explanations to 'cultural' meant that, by the late 1990s and the 2000s, there was a growing influence in youth sociology of post-modernism and identity politics as well as increasing preponderance towards Beck's work on 'choice biographies' and the 'individualisation thesis' (e.g. Du Bois Reymond 1998).

The situation in the antipodes provides a good case in point for the direction of travel described earlier. By the middle of 2000s, class analysis virtually disappears from Australian youth sociology. Wyn and Harris (2004: 282), for example, highlight the distinctiveness of youth sociology in Australia and New Zealand suggesting that researchers should not 'continue to interpret the lives of young people with references to orthodoxies and norms of the past', contending that 'established theoretical traditions' of a particular nation limit the possibilities of other approaches. While this was not an explicit criticism of British class theory, it implied that youth sociology in Australia and New Zealand should move beyond such approaches and recognise both the local context and the way that social change is reconfiguring the lives of the young. Here onwards, Australian youth sociology took a more significant lead in developing a more diverse body of work. For example, the concept of 'social generation' emerged out of Australia as a new conceptual framework that offered alternative ways to read and analyse social change (Wyn and Woodman 2006); class, while notionally discussed, was relegated to the margins (France and Roberts 2015).

There was a 'countermovement' within youth sociology that aimed to reassert class analysis[15] and a number of important studies, such as research by MacDonald and Marsh (2005), illuminated class practices in highly disadvantaged areas, or, in the case of Griffin (2011), argued that class remains important for studies of youth (sub)cultures. Where class is still considered important there is a tendency for it to be constructed around discussions on 'bounded agency' (Evans 2002), and 'structural individualism' (Roberts 2009) or epistemological fallacy (Furlong and Cartmel 2007). Yet, such approaches are limited in their ability to explain the social processes that *shape* class relationships, being used more to try and find a neat solution to contradictions of the growing awareness of 'individualisation'. We would suggest a more useful way of understanding class identities is less about the dichotomy between 'structure and agency' and more about 'social practice' and the process of social reproduction (France et al. 2012).

SOCIOLOGY OF EDUCATION AND THE QUESTION OF CLASS PRIVILEGE

Similar to mainstream sociology, it is important to recognise that much class theorising in youth sociology has given little attention to the rich and wealthy. In mainstream sociology, this 'gap' is well recognised, with much theorising concentrated on those groups seen as 'marginal', 'disadvantaged', 'excluded' or 'poor', with far less attention given to the 'super rich' or elites (Savage 2015). Youth sociologists have always wanted to highlight not only the impact that inequality can and does have on young people's trajectories in life but also how they blamed for their problems. Yet, in this process youth sociology has traditionally given very little attention to how class *operates* across the youth population. Historically, questions have been raised about the lack of attention to 'ordinary youth' (Brown 1987) and more recently, Roberts (2011) has raised the importance of understanding the 'missing middle'. Yet, we also want to argue that the sociology of youth needs to turn its lens to how the wealthy, the advantaged and the privileged not only maintain their own position but also socially reproduce their class futures for their children by transferring wealth, and cultural and social capital across generations. This approach is in line with the argument being developed by Savage (2015) in the UK and is something we believe is a gap in youth studies.

That said, historically and internationally, attempts to bring these matters to attention exist, although most are concentrated in the sociology of education. For example, a number of localised studies within the sociology of education explored how middle-class privilege operates in the education system (Ball 2008). Within this work there has been a particular interest in how middle-class young women in both the public and private schooling sectors are able to 'position' themselves for a life that maintains their social privilege (Walkerdine et al. 2001; Maxwell and Aggleton 2010, Stephen and Gillies 2011). More recently, Kenway and her team have been actively researching how class privilege operates for young women in schooling in Australia (Kenway and Koh 2015; McCarthy and Kenway 2014). Similarly, in New Zealand, Stephen and Gillies (2011) researched how privilege worked for girls in the independent sector, while Thrupp (2007a, b) reminds us how privilege is institutionalised in the educational sector through school zoning and how the mixing of public and private education structures ensure that those from privileged backgrounds continually gain advantage in the New Zealand compulsory education system. While this work starts to increase our understanding of the processes used by the rich and wealthy to advantage their children, there is a tendency to focus attention on white girls and on the compulsory schooling system. Given the reconfiguring of school-to-work transition, more attention must be given to how these processes operate in post-compulsory school environments; something we elude to in Chapter 3.

A Bourdieusian Approach to Social Class

So far we have showed how both mainstream sociology and youth sociology have struggled with centralising the theorising of class, especially in periods of rapid social change. The work of Pierre Bourdieu provides an invaluable way of looking at how social class is socially reproduced. While there exists a growing body of work using Bourdieu's influence, especially in the sociology of education, we see a limited use of his work in other fields or research that tries to show the interconnections between education, training and work. Our objective here is to outline the 'tools' that we think can be of value in this process.

Bourdieu was never explicit about his theory of class, in fact he never engaged with writers such as Goldthorpe and Wright, neither did he attempt to create a typology of classes. He was clear that social scientists could never replicate or identify the 'true' nature of a class as any attempt is a social construction, leaving simply what he called the creation of 'classes on paper' (Bourdieu 1987: 7). But what is different about his work that makes it so appealing? As Atkinson suggests, Bourdieu's approach to class is that it

> is not simply about life chances, even if they come into it, nor is it about exploitation, even if that does follow from it. Instead class is about the fundamental principles of social and cultural difference within a society, the conditions of life tied up with these differences and the power, struggle and domination invested in them. (Atkinson 2015: 61–62)

Bourdieu is interested in what he calls the 'social space' in which 'people are positioned according to their possession of various types of capital and which furnishes them with a habitus, or set of dispositions' (Atkinson 2009: 901). As we shall see in the following 'habitus' and 'capitals' are important here, but its position in social space of Bourdieu's thinking is critical, being an 'objective' position where individuals are located and grouped by 'virtue of their portfolio of economic and cultural capital' (Crossley 2008: 88). Class then is not just about purely economic circumstances such as income or wealth ownership or 'labour market positions' or relationships to 'modes of production', it is also about social and cultural relationships and the struggles for power, influence and domination of one lifestyle over another (Crossley 2008). This is not to say that labour market relationships are not relevant; paid work can be an important and central aspect of a person's habitus (Atkinson 2009). In fact, once we start to map the relationship of capitals in social space we can start to group together individuals who have similar levels of capitals and have an element of proximity. For example, those who have a high volume of economic, cultural and social capital can be seen as holding a similar position and can then be thought to approximate a social class. This proximity in social space is also physical in that it will tend to generate a certain degree of connection and group formation between individuals who are more likely to live and socialise in similar places. Such relationships help social groups to develop similar '...lifestyles, outlooks, dispositions and a tacit sense of place in the world...' (Crossley 2008:93), what Bourdieu then calls a person's 'classed habitus'. So what is habitus? Wacquant argues that it is a

> system of durable and transposable dispositions through which we perceive, judge and act in the world...acquired through lasting exposure to particular social conditions and conditionings via the internalizing of external constraints and possibilities (Wacquant 2006: 267)

These 'dispositions' are seen as being formed in childhood through a *relational dialectic* with the surrounding ecological context of social life (Bourdieu and Wacquant 1992). While habitus is '...endlessly transformed' (Bourdieu 1984: 466), it is seen to be a durable lens in which we see and interpret the world. It is not seen as consciousness, rather something that happens '...below the level of consciousness and language, beyond the reach of introspective scrutiny or control of will' (Bourdieu 1984: 466), that predisposes individuals and helps generate and create strategies to manage everyday life. Habitus, therefore, acts as a form of '...active presence of the past in the present' (Bourdieu 1990: 56) and predisposes individuals in generative and creative ways to develop strategies that maximise profits either economically or symbolically. From this, Bourdieu concludes that habitus is both *structured* by a range of social forces and is also *structuring*, in that it gives coherence and meaning to a number of activities across the life course. One of the consequences of habitus is that it acts to inform us of the 'rules of the game' and how it should be played. Bourdieu suggests that social life is not always consciously or totally planned. It is not simply random, nor is it purely accidental, but much of life 'just happens'. As Williams suggests, the idea of

'...intentionality without intention' or '...knowledge without cognitive intent' is important in creating a 'pre-reflexive subject' (1995: 582). In this context our habitus helps create a sense of logic about how things work. 'Knowing the game' and its 'rules' then enables people to negotiate and manipulate the positional challenges they experience daily. It helps us navigate the social world because our habitus informs us 'how things are done' in particular settings and environments.

Bourdieu's model of habitus has been much criticised as it is seen as remaining either essentially deterministic or at the very least lacking recognition of other factors that may influence choice and action (Alexander 1994; Jenkins 1992). Adams (2006: 515), for example, suggests that '..."agency" is stretched to its limits', suggesting that 'reflexivity' and 'agency' in Bourdieu's model is seemingly ignored or seems to 'sit on the back of the individual', operating to direct individual action. This raises questions over the relevance of habitus in providing us with the central 'lens' to interpret and shape the choices people make. We suggest such interpretations misrepresent Bourdieu's position.

Bourdieu (1992: 133) himself recognised that habitus is '...durable and not eternal!' being '...consistently subjected to experiences, and therefore constantly affected by them in a way that either reinforces or modifies its structure'. He suggests that for many people their experience will continually reaffirm their habitus, yet he also recognises it is most useful in explaining action where normative rules are not explicit (Swartz 1997). If the social context is highly codified or regulated then habitus may not be as influential in structuring responses. This can be relevant to how the 'field' (see the following) is organised and what the person's relationship to it may be. Farrugia (2013: 12), for example, suggests that 'habitus, with its stock of dispositions and embodied capital, gives reflexive practices their content.' In other words, context matters and different contexts and 'fields of practice' (outlined in more detail in the following) shape how a person's habitus is drawn upon in certain situations:

> Times of crisis, in which the routine adjustment of subjective and objective structures is brutally disrupted, constitute a class of circumstances when indeed 'rational choice' may take over, at least amongst those agents who are in a position to be rational. (Bourdieu 1992: 131)

At such times, people must be more strategic and draw upon a wide range of resources: '...habitus has its 'blips', critical moments when it misfires or is out of phase (Bourdieu 2000: 162). Farrugia (2013: 12) elaborates arguing that reflexivity around habitus is strongly related to a person's class position, suggesting that '...reflexive subjectivities emerge in response to local structural conditions and are mobilised in ways that are conditioned by familiar forms of social inequality'.

As we said before, a person's position and relationship to others is strongly influenced by the extent of their capital. Bourdieu sees three types of capital as important. First, Bourdieu, like others before him, sees *economic* capital as majorly significant. This includes not only income differentials but also wealth ownership such as property and other forms of assets (shares/private pensions etc.). Secondly, he sees a person's *cultural* capital. This has a number of dimensions. It refers to 'the ensemble of cultivated dispositions that are internalized by the individual through socialization and that constitute schemes of appreciation and understanding' (Swartz 1997: 76) and is *embodied*. It develops in childhood and is concerned with the cultivation of cultural distinctions. It is concerned with language, art and appreciation of the world around us. It is also concerned with the things we consume and is *objectified* in objects such as the ownership of books and works of art. But it exists also in *institutional* form and especially the educational credential system, where the acquiring of qualifications that are institutionally recognised as symbols of success and achievement.

Important to recognise here is that what is defined as 'legitimate' is in many ways arbitrary but relates to 'high-brow' cultural practices that are *recognised* as 'distinguished' and 'exclusive' (Atkinson 2015: 68–69). The dominant class are separated from the 'choice of necessity' (Bourdieu 1984: 373) that is linked to the conditions of existence of the poor, and they are also able to impose their way of life as the legitimate one because they have the power (and authority) through the media, education and politics to define what is 'good' and what people should aspire to (Bourdieu 1984). In this context the cultural practice of the dominated is usually defined as 'common' and 'vulgar' and is structured by the 'choice of necessity'. The third form of capital is social capital, which Bourdieu defines as

> the sum of the resources, actual or virtual, that accrue to an individual or a group by virtue of possessing a durable network of more or less

institutionalized relationships of mutual acquaintance and recognition. (Bourdieu and Wacquant 1992: 119)

Social capital then is about the range of social networks that people have and accrue over time. They can then be used and mobilised to gain information about opportunities and give access to resources. The classic imagery of this is evoked by the maxim that getting on in the world relies on 'not what you know but who you are'.

What is important to recognise here in thinking about Bourdieu's development of cultural and social capital is his desire to show how these different capitals both interact or operate separately to create a *source of power and influence*. Under certain conditions they can be used and converted into advantage and privilege, especially amongst the dominant classes. As Swartz (1997: 75) claims, Bourdieu's work is the study of 'how and under what conditions individuals and groups employ strategies of capital accumulation, investing and converting kinds of capital in order to maintain or enhance their positions in the social order...'.

Despite Bourdieu stating that we ought not to aim to 'create' classes because they are just classes on paper, his notion of social space allows us to see how social classes can be symbolically constructed and linked to both power and advantage. Bourdieu creates a way of recognising how the combination of capitals can 'position' people in social space. For example, those with high economic, cultural and social capital can be seen to be highly advantaged (compared to those with low). It also permits recognition of possible contradictions in that people can have high cultural capital (e.g. artists) but low economic and social capital, or high economic capital but low cultural capital (the lottery winner from a poor background). This facilitates understanding of how groups are formed around the different relationships to capital.

One interrelated issue around the classed nature of society is brought to our attention through Bourdieu's notion of 'symbolic violence', which 'to put it tersely and simply as possible, is the *violence which is exercised upon a social agent with his or her complicity*' (Bourdieu 1992: 167). This has three interrelated dimensions. He suggests that 'knowledge' such as language, myth, art and ways of appreciating the world exercise as cognitive functions, embedded with symbolic codes, which serve as instruments of domination. He rejects Marx's idea of ideology (Bourdieu and Eagleton 1992) and argues instead for an approach that recognises how language and knowledge is used to legitimatise the social order. He proposes that it is so embedded in our culture and way of life that it normalises the 'status quo' giving recognition to the continuation of inequality and domination of one group over others. People, he suggests, are complicit in this process in that we comply and accept this as normal (Bourdieu and Wacquant 1992). This form of symbolic power is then used to reinforce control and regulation of the disadvantaged. For example, terms such as 'chavs', 'benefit scroungers', the 'underclass' and the 'workshy' can be utilised by the powerful to their own ends (Tyler 2013).

Finally, we cannot ignore the importance of 'fields'. A field is

> a structured social space, a field of forces, a force field. It contains people who dominate and people who are dominated. Constant, permanent relationships of inequality operate inside this space, which at the same time becomes a space in which various actors struggle for the transformation or preservation of the field. (Bourdieu 1998: 40–1)

Fields denote '...arenas of production, circulation and appropriation of goods services, knowledge and status' (Swartz 1997: 117) and it is here where a person's capitals and habitus can be most productive (Bourdieu and Wacquant 1992) offering not only insight into the 'rules of the game' but also the resources to help individuals navigate and manoeuvre themselves to positions of advantage over others. As suggested in the aforementioned quote, fields are sites of struggle, with winners and losers, and those who are better positioned (have more economic, cultural and social capital) in the field will always win. A field is a 'separate universe governed by its own laws...' (Bourdieu 2005: 5) and can be multiple and intersecting. While they are strongly structured by laws and institutional arrangements, they can and are more fluid and dynamic and open to change.

For the purpose of our analysis (in Chapter 3), we propose that we understand and see the area of post-compulsory education, training and employment as a field in its own right (France 2016). While each aspect can be understood as a sub-field, by seeing the three areas as a distinct field in its own right, we can recognise and identify the interconnection between them, showing both the dynamic of this relationship and the way that young people's movement through this stage of the life course is structured and shaped by education, training and employment. We can also trace the continuity of experiences that different social classes have, illuminating and highlighting how longer term outcomes are strongly associated with a range of experiences that emerge within each of the subfields. In this sense

> the social world can be represented as a space (with several dimensions) constructed on the basis of principles of differentiation or distribution constituted by the set of properties active within the social universe in question, i.e., capable of conferring strength, power within that universe, on their holder. Agents and groups of agents are thus defined by their relative positions within that space. (Bourdieu 1985: 724)

Conclusion

This chapter has set down some of the challenges of understanding and analysing class in the UK, Australia and New Zealand. Our view is that much recent criticism of class theory overstates the extent and consequences of social change. As a part of this process, inadvertently, social class becomes marginalised as focus on a rising tide of inequality across all social groups takes centre stage, with structural determinants being deprioritised. While class analysis has 'waxed and waned' over the last 20 years, there is growing recognition that class still matters. In fact, as Skeggs (2015: 206) suggests, '... it is now much harder, even downright embarrassing, to claim class to be redundant or to claim it to be a "zombie category"'. We have suggested that the current state of affairs in youth sociology also needs to recognise this. While emphasis on class has always been claimed to be important, there is limited explicit contemporary theorising of the operation and social reproduction of class and there remains a significant amount of research where it is virtually invisible, being claimed as either irrelevant or at the very least relegated to a less significant status. In the chapters that follow, we document how the tools of Bourdieu help make visible the enduring processes of social reproduction in these 'new' times.

Notes

1. The most influential was the embourgeoisement theory in the 1960s that proposed that growing affluence was reducing the impact of class (Zweig 1961) followed by Andrew Gorz's work (1982) *Farewell to the Working Class*, London Pluto Press and Pakulski and Waters (1996) *The Death of Class*, London, Sage.

2. This is not to say that the claims have gone uncontested. See, for example, the special edition of *Sociology* in 2014.
3. In the UK, 'public' schools are private, fee-paying schools.
4. The Māori land march was led by 80-year-old Whina Cooper, who walked the full length of North Island in protest at the loss of Māori land and the occupation of Bastion Point by local Māori in Auckland; see Carlyon and Morrow (2013) for detailed discussion.
5. The Treaty of Waitangi Tribunal was formed in 1975 to help the state develop future policies that recognised its responsibilities under the treaty. See https://nzhistory.govt.nz/the-treaty-of-waitangi-act-passes-into-law-setting-up-the-waitangi-tribunal for overview.
6. This was used as a proxy for class but it was never seen as a social class measure.
7. Pākehā is a Māori language term for non-Maori or for New Zealanders who are of European descent.
8. This is measured by the sum of total assets minus total liabilities.
9. No such study has yet been done in New Zealand.
10. https://tasayouth.wordpress.com/2014/10/21/hipsters-bogans-and-contemporary-class-anxieties/
11. http://www.nzherald.co.nz/nz/news/article.cfm?c_id=1andobjectid=11764507
12. One response was the development of 'elite theory' (Bottomore 1993), although such an approach has tended to focus on the interrelationship between wealth and political power (Savage 2015) giving limited coverage to the 'super affluent' and their role as a social class.
13. Rodgernomics is a term used in New Zealand similar to 'Thatcherism' in the UK and 'Reaganomics' in the USA. It was created by a New Zealand journalist to describe the economic policies of Roger Douglas after his appointment in 1984 as Minister of Finance. These were strongly influenced by Classical Liberalism.
14. Although this idea has been recently challenged, see Goodwin and O'Connor 2005.
15. See Brannen and Nilsen 2005 and Roberts 2010.

References

Adams, M. (2006). Hybridizing habitus and reflexivity: Towards an understanding of contemporary identity? *Sociology*, *40*(3), 511–528.

Alexander, J. C. (1994). Modern, anti, post, and Neo: How social theories have tried to understand the 'New World' of' our time'. *Zeitschrift Für Soziologie*, *23*(3), 165–197.

Ashton, D. N., & Field, D. (1976). *Young Workers: From School to Work*. London: Hutchinson.
Ashton, D. N., Maguire, M., & Spilsbury, M. (1990). *Restructuring the labour market: The implications for youth*. London: Macmillan.
Atkinson, W. (2009). Rethinking the working-class nexus: Theoretical foundations for recent trends. *Sociology*, *43*(5), 896–912.
Atkinson, W. (2010). The myth of the reflexive worker: Class and work histories in neo-liberal times. *Work, Employment and Society*, *24*(3), 413–429.
Atkinson, W. (2015). *Class*. Cambridge: Polity Press.
Australian Council of Social Services. (2015). *Inequality in Australia; a nation divided*. Strawberry Hills: NSW: Australian Council of Social Services.
Ball, S. J. (2002). *Class strategies and the education market: The middle classes and social advantage*. London: Routledge.
Ball, S. J. (2008). *The education debate: policy and politics in the twenty-first century*. Bristol: Policy Press.
Bates, I., & Riseborough, G. (1993). *Youth and inequality*. Milton Keynes: Open University Press.
Bauman, Z. (2001). *Globalization: The Human Consequences*. New York: Columbia University Press.
Baxter, J., Emmison, M., Western, J., & Western, M. (1991). *Class analysis and contemporary Australia*. Melbourne: Macmillan.
Beck, U., & Beck- Gernsheim, E. (2002). *Individualisation: Institutional individualism and it's social and political consequences*. London: Sage.
Beck, U. (1992). *Risk society: Towards a new modernity*. London: Sage.
Beck, U. (1997). *The Reinvention of Politics*. Cambridge: Polity Press.
Blackman, S. (2005). Youth subcultural theory: A critical engagement with the concept, its origins and politics, from the Chicago school to postmodernism. *Journal of Youth Studies*, *8*(1), 1–20.
Bottomore, T. (1993). *Class and elite theory, elites and society*. London: Routledge.
Bourdieu, P. (1984). *Distinction: A social critique of the judgement of taste*. Cambridge US: Harvard University Press.
Bourdieu, P. (1985). The social space and the genesis of groups. *Theory and Society*, *14*(6), 723–744.
Bourdieu, P. (1987). What makes a social class?. *Berkeley Journal of Sociology*, *32*, 1–17.
Bourdieu, P. (1990). *The logic of practice*. Standford US: Stanford University Press.
Bourdieu, P. (1992). *The Logic of practice*. Cambridge: Polity Press.
Bourdieu, P. (1998). *Practical reason: On the theory of action*. Cambridge: Polity Press.
Bourdieu, P. (2000). *Pascalian meditations*. Stansford: Stanford University Press.
Bourdieu, P. (2005). *The social structures of the economy*. Cambridge: Polity.

Bourdieu, P., & Eagleton, T. (1992). Doxa and common life. *New Left Review*, *1*(191), 111–121.
Bourdieu, P., & Wacquant, L. (1992). *An invitation to reflexive sociology*. Cambridge: Polity.
Brannen, J., & Nilson, A. (2005). Individualisation, choice and structure: A discussion of current trends in sociological analysis. *The Sociological Review*, *53*(3), 412–428.
Brown, P. (1987). *Schooling ordinary kids: Inequality, unemployment, and the new vocationalism*. London: Routledge.
Carlyon, J., & Morrow, D. (2013). *Changing times: New Zealand since 1945*. Auckland, New Zealand: Auckland University Press.
Carter, M. (1966). *Into work*. London: Penguin books.
Connell, R. (1983). Social class in Australia. *Search*, *14*, 247–248.
Connell, R. (2015). Setting sail: The making of sociology in Australia 1955–75. *Journal of Sociology*, *51*(2), 354–369.
Connell, R., & Irving, T. (1980). *Class structure in Australian history*. Melbourne: Longman Cheshire.
Crossley, N. (2008). Social class. In M. Grenfell (Ed.), *Pierre Bourdieu: key concepts*. Abingdon: Routledge.
Crothers, C. (2013). Social class in New Zealand: A review based on survey evidence. *New Zealand Sociology*, *29*(3), 90–127.
Devine, F., Savage, S. J., & Crompton, R. (2005). *Rethinking class: culture, identities and lifestyle*. London: Palgrave Macmillan.
Du Bois-Reymond, M. (1998). I don't want to commit myself yet': Young people's life concepts. *Journal of Youth Studies*, *1*(1), 63–79.
During, S. (1998). Postcolonialism and globalisation: A dialectical relation after all?. *Postcolonial Studies*, *1*, 31–47.
Dwyer, P., Wilson, B., & Woock, R. R. (1984). *Confronting school and work: Youth and class cultures in Australia*. Melbourne: Allen and Unwin.
Evans, K. (2002). Taking control of their lives? Agency in young adult transitions in England and the New Germany. *Journal of Youth Studies*, *5*(3), 245–269.
Falcous, M., & McLeod, C. (2012). Anyone for Tennis? Class and status in New Zealand. *New Zealand Sociology*, *27*(1), 13–30.
Farrugia, D. (2013). Young people and structural inequality: Beyond the middle ground. *Journal of Youth Studies*, *16*(5), 679–693.
Fevre, R. (2007). Employment insecurity and social theory: The power of nightmares. *Work, Employment and Society*, *21*(3), 517–535.
Finn, D. (1987). *Training without jobs: New deals and broken promises*. London: Macmillan Education.
France, A., Bottrell, D., & Armstrong, D. (2012). *A political ecology of youth and crime*. London: Palgrave Macmillan.

France, A. (2016). *Understanding youth in the global economic crisis.* Bristol: Policy Press.
France, A., & Roberts, S. (2015). The problem of social generations: A critique of the new emerging orthodoxy in youth studies. *Journal of Youth Studies, 18*(2), 215–230.
Furlong, A., & Cartmel, F. (2007). *Young people and social change.* Buckingham: Open University Press.
Giddens, A. (1991). *Modernity and self-identity.* Cambridge: Polity Press.
Goldthorpe, J. H. (1980). *Social mobility and class structure in modern Britain.* Oxford: Clarendon Press.
Goldthorpe, J. H. (2002). Globalisation and social class. *West European Politics, 25*(3), 1–28.
Goldthorpe, J. H. (2007). *On sociology; Volume one.* 2nd ed. Stanford: Stanford University.
Goldthorpe, J. H., & McKnight, G. (2006). The Economic Base of Social Class Analysis. In Morgan, S., Grusky, D. B. and Fields, G.S. (ed.), *Mobility and Inequality: Frontiers of Research from Sociology and Economics.* Stanford: Stanford University.
Goodwin, J., & O'Connor, H. (2005). Exploring complex transitions: Looking back at the 'Golden Age' of youth transitions. *Sociology, 39*(2), 201–220.
Gorz, A. (1982). *Farewell to the working class.* London: Pluto.
Graetz, B., & Mcallister, I. (1988). *Dimensions of Australian society.* 1st ed. Melbourne: Macmillan.
Greig, A., Lewins, F., & White, K. (2003). *Inequality in Australia.* Cambridge: Cambridge University Press.
Griffin, C. (1985). *Typical girls?: Young women from school to the job market.* London: Routledge and Kegan Paul.
Griffin, C. E. (2011). The trouble with class: Researching youth, class and culture beyond the 'Birmingham School'. *Journal of Youth Studies, 14*(3), 245–259.
Haverig, A., & Roberts, S. (2011). The New Zealand OE as governance through freedom: Rethinking 'the apex of freedom'. *Journal of Youth Studies, 14*(5), 587–603.
Hobsbawn, E. (1968). *Industry and empire; From 1750 to the present day.* London: Penguin.
Hollands, R. G. (1990). *The Long Transition: Class, culture and youth training.* London: Macmillan Education.
Howard, J. (1996, 18th November). Confront Our Past, yes but let's not become consumed by it. *The Australian.*
Jenkins, R. (1992). *Pierre Bourdieu.* London: Routledge.
Jones, O. (2011). *Chavs: The demonization of the working class.* London: Verso.

Kenway, J., & Koh, A. (2015). Sociological silhouettes of elite schooling. *British Journal of Sociology of Education, 36*(1), 1–10.
MacDonald, R., & Marsh, J. (2005). *Disconnected youth? Growing up in Britain's poor neighbourhoods.* London: Palgrave Macmillan.
Martin, B., & Wajcman, J. (2004). Understanding Class Inequality in Australia. In Devine, F. and Waters, M. (Ed.), *Social Inequalities in Comparative Perspective.* Oxford: Blackwell Publishing.
Maxwell, C., & Aggleton, P. (2010). The bubble of privilege: Young, privately educated women talk about social class. *Journal of Sociology of Education, 31*(1), 3–15.
McCarthy, C., & Kenway, J. (2014). Introduction: Understanding the re-articulations of privilege over time and space. *Globalisation, Societies and Education, 12*(2), 165–176.
McRobbie, A. (1978). Working class girls and femininity. *Women's Studies Group (CCCS), Women Take Issue. Aspect of Women's Subordination, Birmingham.*
Mizen, P. (1995). *The state, young people and youth training: In and against the training state.* London: Mansell.
Nash, R. (2001). Class, ability' and attainment: A problem for the sociology of education. *British Journal of Sociology of Education, 22*(2), 189–202.
Pakulski, J., & Waters, M. (1996). *The death of class.* London: Sage.
Pini, B., McDonald, P., & Mayes, R. (2012). Class contestations and Australian's resources boom: The emergence of the cashed-up bogen. *Sociology, 46*(1), 142–158.
Pitts, D. (1977). *Social class in New Zealand.* Auckland: Longman Paul.
Rashbrooke, M. (Ed.). (2013). *Inequality: A New Zealand Crisis.* Wellington: Bridget Williams Books.
Roberts, K. (1995). *Youth and employment in modern Britain.* Oxford: Oxford University Press.
Roberts, K. (2009). Opportunity structures then and now. *Journal of Education and Work, 22*(5), 355–368.
Roberts, S. (2010). Misrepresenting 'choice biographies'?: A reply to Woodman. *Journal of Youth Studies, 13*(1), 137–149.
Roberts, S. (2011). Beyond 'NEET' and 'tidy' pathways: Considering the 'missing middle' of youth transition studies. *Journal of Youth Studies, 14*(1), 21–39.
Roper, B.. (1997). The changing class structure. In C. Rudd & B. Roper (eds.), *The political economy of New Zealand* (pp. 79–99). New York: OUP.
Savage, M., Devine, F., Cunningham, N., Taylor, M., Yaojun, L., Hjellbrekke, J., Le Roux, B., Friedman, S., & Miles, A. (2013). A new model of social class? Findings from the BBC's great British class survey experiment. *Sociology, 47*(2), 219–250.

Savage, M., Devine, F., Cunningham, N., Friedman, S., Laurison, D., Miles, A., Snee, H., & Taylor, M. (2015). On social class, anno 2014. *Sociology, 49*(6), 1011–1030.
Savage, M. (2015). *Social class in the 21st century*. London: Pelican.
Sheppard, J., & Biddle, N. (2015). *Social class in Australia: Beyond the 'Working' and 'Middle Class'*. ANU: ANU College of Arts and Social Sciences.
Skeggs, B. (2004). *Class, self, culture*. London: Routledge.
Skeggs, B. (2015). Introduction: Stratification or exploitation, domination, dispossession and devaluation?. *The Sociological Review, 63*, 205–222.
Stephens, S., & Gillies, A. (2011). Understanding the role of everyday practices of privilege in the perpetuation of inequalities. *Journal of Community and Applied Social Psychology, 22*, 145–158.
Swales, K. (2016). *Understanding the leave vote*. London: NATcen Social Research.
Swartz, D. (1997). *Power and culture: The sociology of Pierre Bourdieu*. Chicago: University of Chicago Press.
Thompson, E. P. (1963). *The making of the English working class*. London: Pelican.
Thrupp, M. (2001). Education policy and social class in England and New Zealand; an instructional comparison. *Journal of Education Policy, 16*(4), 221–254.
Thrupp, M. (2007a). Education's "Inconvenient Truth' - Part One - Persistent middle class advantage. *New Zealand Journal of Teachers' Work, 4*(2), 77–88.
Thrupp, M. (2007b). Education's "Inconvenient Truth": Part Two - The middle classes have too many friends in education. *New Zealand Journal of Teachers' Work, 5*(1), 54–62.
Tyler, I. (2013). *Revolting Subjects: Social Abjection and Resistance in Neoliberal Britain*. London: Zed books.
Wacquant, L. (2006). Pierre Bourdieu. In R. Stone (Ed.), *Key contemporary thinkers*. London: Macmillan.
Walkerdine, V., Lucey, H., & Melody, J. (2001). *Growing up girl: Psycho-social explorations of gender and class*. London: Palgrave.
Wilkes, C. (1985). *The New Zealand class structure*. Auckland: Massey University.
Wilkes, C. (2004). Class. In Spoonley, P., Pearson, D., and Shirley, I. (eds.), *New Zealand Society: A Sociological Introduction* (2nd ed.). New Zealand: Dunmore Press.
Williams, S. J. (1995). Theorising class, health and lifestyles: Can Bourdieu help us? *Sociology of Health and Illness, 17*(5), 577–604.
Willis, P. (1977). *Learning to labour: How working class kids get working class jobs*. Farnborough: Saxon House.
Wolff, J. (1999). Cultural studies and the sociology of culture. *Contemporary Sociology, 28*(5), 499–507.

Woodman, D. (2009). The mysterious case of the pervasive choice biography: Ulrich Beck, structure/agency, and the middling state of theory in the sociology of youth. *Journal of Youth Studies*, *12*(3), 243–256.

Woodward, I., & Emmison, M. (2009). The Intellectual Reception of Bourdieu in Australian Social Sciences and Humanities. *Sociologica*, *2*(3), 1–22.

Wright, E. O. (1978). *Class, crisis and the state*. London: Verso.

Wyn, J., & Harris, A. (2004). Youth research in Australia and New Zealand. *Young*, *12*(3), 271–289.

Wyn, J., & Woodman, D. (2006). Generation, youth and social change in Australia. *Journal of Youth Studies*, *9*(5), 495–514.

Zweig, F. (1961). *The worker in affluent society: Family life and history*. London: Heinemann.

CHAPTER 3

Education, Social Mobility and the Enduring Nature of Class

Abstract In recent decades, the 'massification' of education and training has seen young people's pathways into adulthood dramatically changed, with the 'school-to-work' model of transition being reconfigured. The question remains, however, whether or not the expansion of post-compulsory education provides the means for social and personal enhancement and increased opportunities for social mobility, or if instead it promotes the status quo, maintaining and reinforcing inequalities through a process of social reproduction. In this chapter we suggest the latter, in that a range of evidence, including that influenced by the work of Pierre Bourdieu, shows that even with such high levels of social change the post-compulsory sub field still serves to perpetuate inequality rather than alleviate it. Class therefore remains a critical feature of how young people experience post-compulsory education and training.

Keywords Massification · Higher education · Vocational education · Graduate · Aspiration · Habitus and capital

THE 'NORMALISATION' OF POST-COMPULSORY EDUCATION

A central ambition of educational policy reform across advanced economies over the last four decades has been, in theory, to democratise the system. Whether motivated by ideas of social emancipation or the need to respond to the shift to a perceived 'knowledge economy', the move from

© The Author(s) 2017
A. France, S. Roberts, *Youth and Social Class*,
DOI 10.1057/978-1-137-57829-7_3

an elite activity to a majority experience is nowhere more pronounced than in post-compulsory education settings. It is here that we find the subjects of interest for this book: youth is intimately tied up with education; indeed, as Mizen notes (2004) education is one of the starkest moments of youth's political and social construction. It is also here, beyond the compulsory phase, where we find substantial markers of change: participation has expanded upwards through the age range and outwards in respect of widening access to larger proportions of populations. Until the 1970s, large proportions of people in industrialised nations left school at age 15 or 16, for the most part moving into paid employment pretty much *en masse*. A relative few, often from privileged families, made up the number of people who stayed at school or college for another year of two, and fewer still went on to university. Nowadays, across almost all OECD countries, upper secondary attainment is the norm. On average, 74% of 25–64-year-olds have achieved this level, compared with 82% for 25–34-year-olds (OECD 2013). Some countries have seen dramatic increases in upper secondary attainment rates from generation to generation. In Chile, Greece, Italy, Korea, Portugal and Spain upper secondary attainment rates for 25–34-year-olds are at least 30 percentage points higher than for older adults (55–64-year-olds).

The post-16 domain in education and training has now become a central field of practice for the young (France 2016). The drivers of this shift are multiple and complex, and they have a long history. For the sake of brevity, we contain the majority of our detailed discussion to policy developments in the last 25 years or so – a period characterised by intensive neoliberal prioritisations that have cemented managerialism, market forces and competition between institutions, and indeed students, as fundamental to the system, all the while further commodifying post-compulsory education, shifting it rhetorically and practically from a public good to a product for individual consumption; a private choice, but one that in many ways becomes ever more compulsory.

Yet, it is worth noting that the drivers underpinning many of the changes in education participation are part of a much longer legacy. In the UK, for instance, we cannot separate entirely developments in participation in the post-compulsory sector from numerous increases in the school-leaving age occurring in England from 1870 through to the latest changes in 2015; indeed, though it often gets lost in contemporary discussion, we can go back to the 1918 Fisher Act to observe the first piece of legislation that at least made provisions for young people to remain in education until 18 years old. Changes in the school-leaving age or other education policy developments often corresponded with or were followed by policies aimed at expanding the post-compulsory sector. We see this, again in the UK, through the 1950s and 1960s where efforts to institute comprehensive education were complemented by a hitherto unprecedented growth of universities and an expansion of what were to become polytechnic, non-university providers of degree-level qualifications to meet growing demand for post-compulsory education.

Another well-noted example is the collapse of youth labour markets, which occurred in the UK, Australia and New Zealand alongside other countries in the early 1980s (France 2016). With the relatively straightforward school-to-work transition of previous years no longer the reliable option, governments responded by rolling out a series of youth training schemes. These and a further expanded further education (FE) sector were sometimes described as efforts at 'warehousing' (Roberts 1995), tenuously tied to an agenda for skill enhancement while for the most part ensuring that young people were not part of the formal unemployment statistics. During the 1980s, growth in post-compulsory education participation was rapid (Clark 2002), followed by a period of stagnation in the 1990s, then another upturn in the early 2000s. Participation in at least some form of post-compulsory education became highly normalised as part of 'the socially constructed and historically derived common base of knowledge, values and norms for action that people grow into and come to take as a natural way of life' (Hodkinson 1998: 304).

The socially and politically constructed aspect of this norm is important to unpack. Here we briefly describe the policy developments in UK, Australia and New Zealand by way of examples of how these processes come to shape and construct such norms (for a fuller account see France 2016). In addition to constraints on space, there is very much a theoretical purpose for limiting the following paragraphs to a discussion of policy developments since the 1990s. During this period, what can be described as the skills agenda, and its attendant policies, has been a crucial component of the growth of post-compulsory education. The skills agenda is a direct response to and intended to enhance transitions from industrial-based economy to a knowledge-based economy. Simultaneously, it is a product of the neoliberal imperative of responsibilising the individual subject to take educational matters into their own hands.

During the mid-1990s, OECD countries were thought to be relatively uniformly 'more strongly dependent on the production, distribution and use of knowledge than ever before' (OECD 1996: 9). Moving from an industrialised era to a post-Fordist economy, premised on high-level products and services and high-end technologies, was expected to herald a new era: an expansion among high level, high skill jobs; a steady number of intermediate, technical skilled roles and a diminishing lower end of the labour market, where low skills and low wages would gradually disappear. It was argued that employment in knowledge-based economies would be underpinned by increasing demand for more highly skilled workers (OECD 1996), who would emerge as countries shifted towards being a 'learning society' to meet the needs of the much heralded, new knowledge economy. In the UK, New Labour's rise to government in 1997 saw a first term in office underpinned by a now rather famous commitment to 'education, education, education'; this commitment's relationship to the knowledge economy was quickly made clear, with the first Minister for Lifelong Learning suggesting that

> If we do *not* create a learning society—if we do *not* find the means of generating the appropriate skills and craft and expertise, then we will fail to develop our most important resource—our people—and we will fail as an economy in this increasingly globalised market. (Kim Howells 1997, original emphasis)

A de-industrialised economy, it was argued, needed a highly skilled, flexible workforce to best serve the requirements of technology and service-based employment (DfEE 1998). Similar arguments took place in Australia and New Zealand in the late 1990s. For example, the Australian Federal Government had seen the necessity of expanding post-16 education, and strongly focussed on increasing university participation numbers (Gale and Tranter 2011). Such expansions saw university enrolment in Australia increase by 15% between 2003 and 2008 and a further 23% between 2008 and 2013 (Peacock et al. 2014). In New Zealand, major restructuring of the higher education sector had been in place since the late 1980s. New Zealand went through significant reconfiguration of its economy following the economic crisis it faced as a result of the UK entering the European market and the global oil crisis in the 1970s. Yet it also identified investment in skills and the knowledge economy as central to its development. By 2003, the then Labour government argued for young people to have the 'new' skills for the high-skilled knowledge economy. This saw the higher education sector continue to grow and expand to unprecedented levels (Grey and

Scott 2012). However, over the last decade or so, and despite becoming embedded in education and economic policy, and perhaps in the wider public consciousness, in countries such as the UK, Australia and New Zealand, the notion of the knowledge economy has been heavily criticised by a wide range of academic research (Brown et al. 2011).

The Vocational Training Sector

The growth of education and training has, of course, not been confined to higher education. Across OECD countries, national governments have increased the pathways and routes (and provision) into vocational training. These have seen the 're-instatement' of apprenticeships or 'on the job' training programmes. For example, New Zealand increased it apprenticeships annually between 1995 and 2008, and despite a drop throughout the early parts of the GFC, it has since continued to increase (France 2016). Similarly in Australia, the expansion of technical and further education (TAFE) institutions and courses has increased over the last 20 years. In 2006, over 1.8 million people took vocational training courses across Australia and this continued to grow year on year until 2013 (France 2016). At its heart has been apprenticeships. These grew by 28% between 2004 and 2012, and while more recently they have been in decline, they still remain a core component of Australian training programmes (France 2016). In the UK, apprenticeships growth continued until 2013 with around 500,000 per year being funded by government (France 2016), and while the number of these have slowly declined as a result of the recent austerity programmes, the industries that provide apprenticeships have been broadened to include the service and hospitality sector. Another major development has been the growth of the 'non-academic' qualification market where diploma's and certificates are considered more relevant in these tough economic times and especially for helping the young unemployed or low skilled get into work (Ainley and Allen 2010; Tomlinson 2013). While governments have focussed on getting young people to gain almost any form of qualification, little attention has been given to the types of jobs young people are able to access. In fact, the key focus is on getting young people to find *any* work to ensure they are not a financial cost to the state (Ainley and Allen 2010). Jobs have been, however, thinner on the ground in recent years, as high youth unemployment levels across OECD countries attest. Yet, the focus from governments has remained on the supply of qualifications rather than stimulating job demand.

As a result a raft of programmes have been developed in the UK, Australia and New Zealand that aim to increase either the 'basic skills' of the unemployed or to 'upskill' and 'reskill' the employed (Tomlinson 2013; and Ainley and Allen 2010). These programmes focus on skills development concerned with 'employability' such as how to get work, how to be 'job ready' and how to manage the risk and uncertainty that now exists in the labour market (Tomlinson 2013). This growth in 'education for employability' (Ainley and Allen 2010: 41), where knowledge becomes replaced by a narrow focus on job skills and life skills, is expanding in the vocational education and training (VET) sectors of the UK, Australia and New Zealand. The new language of VET concentrates on concepts such as 'competency training' and 'learning outcomes,' which then bring about a radical change in educational curricula that shift the emphasis in outcomes towards 'employability' skills. Schools, especially those with low-attainment levels, along with FE colleges that take the academically 'unsuccessful' and those institutions that target poor or problematic populations have increased these types of strategies (Allais 2012), facilitating the embedding and normalising of 'employability' skills within a wide range of educational institutions.

While continued 'skill acquisition' is now seen as a necessity for all young people, VET providers also operate to 'warehouse' many of the unemployed and low income earners. The process of 'churning' between employability qualification programmes and low-paid work is becoming common practice (Tomlinson 2013). This has seen the creation of a system largely concerned with managing the unemployed when work remains scarce. VET courses have been left to '...fill the vacuum left by the decline in youth jobs and traditional industrial apprenticeships that arise as a result of the post-industrial changes' (Ainley and Allen, 2010: 41). This is a feature of how youth policies have historically managed the growth of underemployment among the young working class.

Of course, VET courses have also always been unattractive to the middle classes as they do not provide routes into middle-class jobs. For example, Ken Roberts (1995) showed in the 1990s those who undertook A-levels were mainly from non-manual backgrounds. The horizon for action available to these young people, therefore, is likely to have led them towards an academic route. It also not only ensured that more vocational pathways were unattractive but also actually perceived as a non-option. This happens because 'horizons for action both limit and enable our view of the world and the choices we can make within it' (Hodkinson 1998: 304).

Massive inequities persist in the segmentation of vocational and academic pathways. Evidence from the UK, Australia and New Zealand all show that the VET sectors are full of those from the lower SES groups (usually the bottom three). Very few middle class or young people from rich families take this route to employment. Despite an emphasis on training, the sector predominantly leads to lower level skills and low pay (France 2016). Australia sees a clear role for TAFE training to open up opportunities in the university sector, yet clear blockages exist. When young people do undertake vocational training in universities it is in the lower-ranked, lesser-esteemed universities rather than the elite universities, which would likely better enhance future prospects (Wheelahan 2008). Further, once students are embedded in vocational training they become 'locked' into a pathway that is hard to escape (Wheelahan 2008). Similar problems exist in the UK where, historically, processes in FE colleges have limited equity rather than increased it for working-class students (Parry et al. 2012). As Bourdieu would remind us, positions in the field are objectively defined by the way it is structured and the way power and resources are distributed (Wheelahan 2008: 263). In this context, neither TAFE nor the UK system is able to address equity issues, only re-enforce class inequality and contribute to social reproduction of working-class transitions to work. Sadly, just like the early 1990s (Bates and Riseborough 1993), social reproduction of working-class trajectories into low-skilled and low-paid work remain a major feature of vocational training. Both upward social mobility and to an extent even sideways mobility stagnate because of the way the field is organised.

The Graduate Market for Jobs

One principal critique centres on issues of supply and demand of the highly skilled 'knowledge worker'. Education policy is charged with, indeed almost entirely focussed upon, enhancing the numbers of people with improved skills and qualifications (in no small part through the management of aspiration, which we address in the following). This is a central component in the human capital thesis – that is that increasing credentials and developing knowledge will enhance economic performance. However, this thesis is highly contested. Keep and Mayhew (2010), for example, outline that investment in human capital (or skill development) cannot change the structure of the labour market. Coffield (1999: 483) neatly explains that '...at its most obvious, highly educated and trained personnel need jobs commensurate with their abilities if they are to boost productivity'. 'Learning society' rhetoric presupposes that this is the case.

Policy makers have been accused of stubbornly ignoring evidence produced by the sociology of education, with Brown (2013) noting that while governments may rhetorically speak of a fairer society created through social mobility, this cannot be achieved. First, there is not unlimited room at the top of labour markets in contemporary societies in ways that were heralded by the promise of the knowledge economy and which were prevalent in the immediate post-war period. Brown (2013: 681) refers to the 'inconvenient truth' of sociological evidence, which is 'that the high rates of mobility achieved in the second half of the twentieth century are explained by 'absolute' changes in the occupational structure, rather than from a narrowing of inequalities in life-chances', and this is a logic implied by many others in sociology more generally (Goldthorpe and Jackson 2007) and the sociology of youth specifically (Berrington et al. 2016).

The reality of the contemporary economy is that technology has replaced many tasks of mid-level jobs. This has led to an expansion in jobs requiring high-level skills in highly technological industries and financial services (France 2016), but there has also been commensurate expansion in low-level, low-pay, low-skilled jobs in the service sector such as stacking shelves, checkout roles, waiting tables and cleaning jobs. Advanced economies – including UK, New Zealand and Australia – now resemble something of an hourglass shape. This kind of labour market is characterised as being polarised between 'lovely and lousy jobs' (Goos and Manning 2007).

The knowledge economy rhetoric is also complicated by the fact that, even within knowledge-intensive industries, less than the majority are defined as 'high knowledge' workers. For example, just 42% of EU employees could be classified as 'high knowledge-skilled'. The remaining 58% are employed in lower levels roles such as porters, cleaners, secretaries and gardeners. Labour Force Surveys, upon which such data are based, count all those people working in an organisation, paying no attention to occupational or hierarchical differences or knowledge-skilled levels (Brine 2006). The implications of this are quite stark. As education policy has encouraged and facilitated the 'massification' of the higher education system, job polarisation has forced more graduates to seek jobs for which they are 'overqualified', and accept lower wages than their qualifications would be expected to garner (Green and Zhu 2010), in a process Brown 2013 calls this 'social congestion'. This influx of 'overqualified' workers in low-skilled jobs has, therefore, blunted wage growth at the bottom of the earnings distribution, despite the growth in demand for workers in these jobs (Goos and Manning 2007).

As noted before, governments have committed to upskilling the general population, and several policy interventions seem to imply this remains an imperative (e.g. Leitch Review of Skills in 2006 in the UK, the Tertiary Education Strategy (TES) 2014–2019 in New Zealand and the Bradley Review in Australia 2008). These have had very variable results, with outcomes being highly stratified according to social characteristics. In the last 30 years, unprecedented rates of staying on in further and higher education have given us a more educated workforce overall. As a result of these cohorts coming through the education system, where for instance in 2006 the UK was home to 2.5 million economically active adults with no qualifications, by 2020 it is estimated that this number will be just 585,000. Crucially, however, these supply side initiatives have not stimulated a corresponding demand. By 2020 the UK economy will still likely have around 7 million jobs that require no entry qualifications (Lawton 2009). We explore this in further detail in Chapter 4.

The key issue here, however, is that whether there is sufficient room at the top to foster and tolerate higher rates of absolute mobility is not the measure of fairness in a society. Indeed, Brown calls this the 'fallacy of fairness' and his wider dissatisfaction with the political agenda of social mobility is documented in his frustration with how little is being done to 'address inequalities in life-chances in a positional struggle for a livelihood' (Brown 2013). A greater sense of fairness can be observed when there are changes to the *relative* chances of enhanced social mobility of those born into different social classes, regardless of how the class or occupational structure may change over time (Brown 2013).

WINNERS AND LOSERS: ENDURING CLASS INEQUALITY IN POST-16 EDUCATION

Our plan here is to discuss a variety of research evidence to show how social class inequalities in post-16 education persist, restrict the levelling of life chances and promote social reproduction. These inequalities not only emerge in terms of the drivers that overwhelmingly steer working-class young people towards 'lesser' valued vocational trajectories, but also to show that when working-class young people do end up on more 'legitimate' academic route to university, they remain subjected to, on the whole, a system that is *designed* for middle-class interests and supporting middle-class privilege. This results in much-differentiated experience and outcomes. We start then by considering the issue of the university social class participation gap. As noted at the outset of this chapter, participation rates in tertiary education have expanded dramatically across most industrialised societies; yet, it is important to recognise that the desire and effort of governments in the UK, Australia and New Zealand to 'widen participation' has had little impact on diversifying participation across SES groups (France 2016). This is not to say that changes have not occurred in the demographics. For example, one aspect of the massification of higher education in particular has been the increased numbers of young women entering university, a point we will return to in Chapter 5. But when it comes to the relative gap in participation, social class differences remain stark. For example, recent UK statistics show that the proportion of higher education participants receiving free school meals (often used as an indicator of working-class status[1]) is around 17–18 percentage points lower, as it has been for the best part of a decade (BIS 2015). There has been some narrowing of the participation gap between students from the highest and lowest income quintiles, but it remains large at over 37 percentage points (Crafword and Greaves 2015).

In Australia, similar patterns can be found. The participation rates of the low SES groups remained stubbornly low at approximately 15% of the total share of higher education between 1993 and 2007 (Bradley et al. 2008). A small increase occurred under the widening participation programmes of the Rudd government, up to 17% by 2012 and holding stable through to 2015, although the low SES groups have higher attrition rates than other groups (Edwards and McMillan 2015). In New Zealand, understanding participation rates is hampered by the lack of quality data, although a recent study (Strathdee and Engler 2012) showed that being from a low SES group decreased the likelihood of higher education participation. In addition, this was complicated when issues such as ethnicity are included (a theme we pick up in Chapter 5). Other indicators also tell significant stories about the role of social class and its associated capital resources, with Australian research showing that men with a university-educated father to be 2.8 times more likely to participate, and women with a university-educated father 3.7 times more likely than other women (Chesters and Watson 2013). The classed nature of universities is also visible in other national-level indicators. For example, young people from low SES are grouped in particular universities. For example, low SES students in Australia tend to 'stay local' and go to universities near to home to help reduce higher education costs and/or they attend universities where they are more likely to find people of similar backgrounds. This pattern is replicated in the UK where 'new' universities such as Teesside, Derby and the University of East London are dominated by local students from low SES groups (France 2016). Middle-class parents who have been to university know what counts and what universities (and course) to avoid. Changes in fees structures also have had an impact. While recently imposed increases in student fees in the UK did not look to have had an especially pronounced effect on participation rates[2]; those from lower participation neighbourhoods were 20% more likely to choose to study near to home, and to live at home while studying, than those from the highest participation neighbourhoods (Artess et al. 2014). It is also worth reasserting that when it comes to participation rates in the VET sector the middle-class are fundamentally missing. These education and training courses are traditionally full of young people from low SES sectors (Wheelahan 2008).

Finally, intake into elite universities of SES students is even more disproportionately low. Despite differences in costs, finance options and admission procedures between countries, institutions such as Oxford and Cambridge in the UK, Harvard and Yale in the USA and the G08 in Australia have very few students from low SES groups. For example, low SES groups are almost three times more likely to go to regional universities in Australia (28.7%) with only 9.6% of students from low SES groups attending at the G08 universities.[3] Similarly, odds of a child at a UK state secondary school who is eligible for free school meals in Year 11 being admitted to Oxbridge by the age of 19 is almost 2,000 to 1 against. By contrast, the odds of a privately educated child being admitted to Oxbridge are 20 to 1 (Social Mobility and Poverty Commission 2013). This is because the elite know that getting into these universities will give their children more income and access to some of the top jobs. For example, a recent report in Australia showed that those studying at one of the G08 universities were likely to earn significantly more over a 40-year career, with an earnings advantage of 6% (Norton 2015). Education and training choices are embedded in different kinds of biographies and different opportunity structures linked closely to young people's classed position (Ball et al. 2002).

The previous information outlines reality of class differences and how they are so entrenched in education and training structures, but there are important questions around why this is the case. A growing body of research into higher educational settings, influenced by the work of Bourdieu, has offered opportunities to develop a more nuanced understanding of how social class still permeates issues that appear to be emblematic of the contemporary requirement for active, agent-led negotiation (France and Roberts 2015). Accordingly, in the following passages we address a series of issues on the theme of class-based difference, by highlighting how the work of Bourdieu produces a lens into the way it operates. Our analysis examines decision-making processes in respect of participating, access to (different types of) institutions, the experience of being a university student and also looks at how access to university resources as well as effective mobilisation and accumulation of capitals can be observed as having a steep class gradient.

A Lack of Aspiration?

The long-standing, low higher education participation among low SES students has often been framed in relation to a lack of aspiration for university among young people from working-class backgrounds. Academic research has sought to distance itself from simplistic aspiration deficit explanations, yet even the most discerning of researchers have documented how most middle-class young people tend to evidence 'deeply normalised grammars of aspiration' (Ball et al. 2002: 69). Such perspectives on grammars and vocabularies of aspiration have been important for the formulation of educational policy in the UK and Australia. Increasing individual 'aspirations' as a part of improving the human capital of the young has been seen as central to economic and social inclusion policies (Seller et al. 2011). This is part of the neoliberal requirement for citizens to be '... held responsible for making consumer choices to maximise their opportunities, in contrast to the previous "politics of expectation", which placed onus on the state to ensure citizens received the equal outcomes to which they were entitled' (Raco 2009: 438). A similar shift has taken place in Australia with the expansion of the 'aspirational voter' in policy debate over the past decade (Johnson 2004). The UK's New Labour government's time in office until 2010 was characterised by sizeable investments of economic and political energy aimed at increasing aspirations of parents and children (Holloway and Pimlott-Wilson 2011), notably through the programme 'AimHigher'. This political discourse essentially argued that to be upwardly socially mobile, working-class young people must learn to 'aspire' like their middle-class peers. This has been a view widely held across the political spectrum (Berrington et al. 2016), with even teachers being observed to be part of the apparatus that position young people and their parents as holding low aspirations (Holloway and Pimlott-Wilson 2011).

This view has been challenged as lacking nuance and perpetuating a myth (St Clair and Benjamin 2013), and argued to represent what Bourdieu refers to as *doxic* knowledge: accepted as self-evident truth and lacking critical scrutiny. Roberts and Evans (2013) argue that rather than having 'low or no aspirations', young British people have a set of aspirations that *make sense to themselves*, but which the political class deem illegitimate or inadequate. This, as Morrison (2014: 125) notes, means that despite the '...social progressiveness and emancipatory potential' of widening access and aspiration enhancing programmes the result is '...social coercion of higher education study is presumed to be the only show in town'.

Sellar et al. (2011), analysing the Australian context, argue strongly that, even if there is an increase in getting students through the doors of Higher Education Institutions, failing to observe and give weight to aspirations that do not wholly correspond with middle-class norms serves to undermine institutions' efforts at producing 'knowledge workers'. The aspirations deficit discourse is, in Australia, New Zealand and the UK, consistent with the dominant neo-liberal approach in the last four decades, which has linked economic governance to individual behaviour, and promoted *particular* 'choices' and self-responsibilisation. This deficit approach runs into further tricky waters when we observe the data on aspirations.

In the UK, Berrington et al. (2016) show that, despite an education aspiration gap between young children according to social class, the *majority* of 10–15-year-olds in all social groups aspire to go to university. The significant contrast is the gap between levels of aspiration and realisation of higher education participation for working-class young people. Meanwhile, Gore et al. (2015) report only very small differences by SES in occupational aspiration in their survey of over 3000 young people. The majority of all groups consistently aspired to professional roles. Tellingly, the justification for these aspirations differs, with low SES (working class) groups framing their aspiration for professional roles as predicated on financial returns, whereas high SES groups (upper middle class) stipulated 'passion' or interest as their motivations. There are of course huge gaps in realising these aspirations – and we agree with Bok's (2010) account from her Australian case study that shows the capacity to aspire in particular ways is a cultural artefact. Habitus and cultural capital work in tandem for middle-class young people to articulate and realise their aspirations, making working-class youth appear to have less than substantive aspirations when the reality is that achieving them is the biggest stumbling block.

A more relevant explanation that informs part of this 'participation gap' is to do with access to elite schooling. From Ball's 2003 study of how middle-class parents strategise to maximise their children's opportunities within the school setting, other research has showed how this goes beyond simply pressuring the school or teachers (see Koh and Kenway 2016 for a mass of international evidence on this). Hansen (2014), for example, shows that parents are prepared to pay significantly more to buy a house located near to better performing primary schools, even before their children reach school-starting age. The link between better schools and higher house prices is now 'one of the most stable empirical regularities' (Gibbons 2012: np), and occurs with similar magnitude worldwide (examples include Machin and Salvanes 2016 on Norwegian high Schools; Feng and Lu 2013 on Chinese high schools). It is a process that reinforces school segregation and inequalities in performance and achievement, and reduces social mobility across the generations. To mobilise economic resources in this fashion for working-class parents would be a struggle, perhaps almost unthinkable. This acts as a powerful reminder that although access to and conversion of various types of cultural capital aids the middle classes in obtaining advantage in the educational field, economic capital remains immensely influential. This is, of course, also identifiable in respect of parent's capacity and desire to pay tuition fees to access the best independent and/or private schools, rather than have their children engage with state-supported provision – a practice of public withdrawal long held in Australia (Campbell et al. 2009) and the UK (Ball 2003). The Australian system is even more stratified in terms of 'choice', with its market-based approach ensuring not just large differences in school tuition costs between regional and metropolitan areas and between state territories but also between public, catholic and private provision, which generally reflect low, medium and higher fees respectively. The fees for a catholic school education are typically 3–4 times higher than for a state school, while private education is around 8 times that of a state education. Among each category there is considerable variation in fees. Being able to access choice in this market is significant for the perpetuation of inequality, because, as Kenway (2013: 303) notes in the Australian context, there is a 'funnelling of a disproportionate percentage of students from the independent school sector into mental labour and a disproportionate percentage of students from the government sector into manual labour'. Elite schools by their very design, of course, are preoccupied in many ways with the maintenance of already entranced advantage (Kenway 2013).

UNIVERSITY IS 'NOT FOR PEOPLE LIKE ME': THE ROLE OF HABITUS

Although not easy to untangle from aspiration, attainment appears to be a better predictor of higher education participation, and shows a strong gradient according to socio-economic status (Strand 2014). Bourdieu's (1973) argument that middle-class families tend to possess greater amounts of symbolic and material resources which they can draw upon to enable them to gain advantages for their members makes sense in this context. That is to say:

> parents from higher social class backgrounds socialise their children in ways compatible with educational success: for example exposing them to legitimised culture, transmitting positive attitudes towards value of education, helping them with their school work and engaging with their teachers and school. (Berrington et al. 2016: 735)

We should not, however, consider working-class parents and children to be in deficit. Instead, because '...identities are continually in the process of being *reproduced as responses to social positions*' (Skeggs 1997: 94, our emphasis; see also; Savage 2000), we must observe that working-class subjectivities (indeed all subjectivities) are a *relational* artefact – people use relational comparisons to define themselves. So, the important and much-observed notion that working-class students' habitus positions university as 'not for people like me' (Archer et al. 2007; Reay et al. 2005) tells only part of the story. The development of this habitus is not simply an attitude passed down from parents or developed via osmosis through interaction with one's class-based peers or social surroundings, but it somehow produces an actor who 'lacks knowledge' of the system and/

or who fears how to best navigate a foreign field. This is part of the issue, but processes of exclusion and alienation experienced in school, but also more widely in the 'symbolic economy', contribute to the development of one's habitus. It is unsurprising, therefore, that when young people attend what they *know* to be relatively less desirable schools, and when they come to feel worthless in the school setting, they experience a sense of inferiority that is entirely compatible with considering higher education seeing an ostensibly middle-class space as off limits (Archer et al. 2007). This is not just because they lack the knowledge of how to access higher education, but because it is recognised as an exclusionary 'social other', and they are cognisant of their exclusion from that place. Their behaviour and associated rejection of higher educational settings and trajectories then becomes a double bind, with investments in style and attitudes that are responses to being culturally excluded (Archer et al. 2007) serving to reinforce those very processes of exclusion, self-perpetuating the stereotype of themselves as lacking in value and 'fit' with the higher education field. This idea of being constructed as lacking and then adopting this mantle with consequent investment in ways of being that reproduce inequality has a long standing in sociology, and resonates strongly with Willis's (1977) formulation of the ways that working-class kids disengaged from education and ended up in working-class jobs; rather than being a new phenomenon, older class processes seem to operate in seemingly new times (Smyth and Banks 2012; Stahl 2015).

Access to higher education provision is highly stratified, but researchers have also documented how experience of university is highly differentiated (Forsyth and Furlong 2000). University study is an option imbued with risks for working-class students in ways that are different for their middle-class peers, whether that is culturally, socially or financially (Archer et al. 2003). These risks are clear when considering young people's choices of institution, which are often highly circumscribed by social class background. Boliver's (2013) recent quantitative analysis shows that applicants from lower class backgrounds and from UK state schools remain much less likely to even apply to elite universities than their *comparably qualified* counterparts from higher social class backgrounds. Studies into the processes that result in such outcomes demonstrate how young working-class people's sense of entitlement to higher education entry is undermined by a diminishing sense of the right to access middle-class spaces and institutions (Reay et al. 2005; see also Donnelly 2015). This echoes the results of studies during the 1990s, which highlighted the relationship between social class and educational choices and pathways (e.g. Reay and Ball 1998; Whitty and Edwards 1998), and this divide continues today (Savage 2015). Choice-making mechanisms, for example, came to significantly bear on the working-class young women studied by Evans (2009). She documents how class and gender combine to produce a habitus that has particular consequences for the location of the institution of choice, predominantly preferring to remain closer to home in order to retain their wider contribution to familial caring roles and duties which often go overlooked and might instead be presumed to be the province of mothers (such as a role, however small, in caring for elder relatives or younger siblings). Simultaneously, elite institutions were viewed as middle-class (often masculine) spaces from which working-class girls are symbolically excluded. In Evans' research, comments about elite institutions feeling like 'Hogwarts' because of formal dinners, the attire of teaching staff (e.g. gowns), paintings of old middle-class white men were common place. A further dimension implicated in choice making, then, is whether students feel able to avoid feeling 'othered' and isolated by and within an institution and also the ways they might be made to feel they 'belong' (Read et al. 2003). The nuances of these processes become clear in Mullen's (2009) research in the USA, which shows that concerns about elitism led students from less privileged backgrounds to consider a place at Ivy League prestigious institutions as out of the realm of the possible. This contrasted strongly with students from wealthy backgrounds whose choice of an Ivy League university place functioned more as an expectation, normalised by parental ideals and explicit high school positioning. Research on peer group networks also shows these tend to be derived from similar class backgrounds (Papapolydorou 2014), which is again implicated in these choice-making mechanisms. As such, elite institutions often become a non-choice, even where working-class students have sufficient grades to achieve entry.

Beyond Access: Higher Education as Class Based Experience

Beyond access to and choices of university, the *lived experience* of higher education is highly classed (Crozier et al. 2008). To begin, pedagogic processes sometimes inhibit or constrain working-class students' engagement (Crozier and Reay 2011). Other UK-based research has also evidenced how '...becoming and being a student are highly differentiated by class' through drawing attention to '...university decision-making processes, funding strategies, and struggles to compete with middle-class peers' (Bradley and Ingram 2013: 68). Ultimately, during university, as a result of middle-class advantage over privileged access to, accrual of and deployment of valued capitals, social inequalities are compounded rather than alleviated (Bathmaker et al. 2013).

Emphasising social difference – and indeed inequalities – takes many forms, with research providing a diverse base for us to understand the multifaceted impact of social class, both in terms of how young working-class people fare relatively badly and how middle-class young people remain advantaged. Lehmann (2012) shows those lacking in sufficient economic and social resources face exclusion from culturally enriching extra-curricular activity and so have long-standing inequalities reinforced. This entrenched social reality has been documented in other research projects, too (see Bradley and Ingram 2013; Bathmaker et al. 2013), and quantitative evidence identifies that such activity is the domain of the middle classes (Purcell et al. 2013). Often, even financial resources will not suffice; Allen and Hollingworth (2013) and Eikhof and Warhurst (2013), for instance, consider how middle-class young people are able to deploy a range of social, cultural and economic resources to access placements in the creative industries. These are *required* efforts to try to stand out from peers in a period of social congestion, produced by a complex amalgam of political decisions and social processes (Brown 2013). Brown argues that this requirement to navigate congested terrain is also a problem for middle classes, too; crucially, however, accruing the right capitals to do well in such a positional competition is not a level-playing field. Therefore, while Brown and others note that the middle classes are increasingly engaged in a secret war for positional advantage, it is working-class young people and their families who suffer from the widening social distance between what is required to do a job, as opposed to what is required to get a *good* job.

Young working-class people have also been observed to suffer from 'closure' behaviours of class-based groups. This prevents proper integration into the university setting and constrains development of social capital, potentially undermining equality of experience (Keane 2011). Even where more 'successful' working-class experiences have been documented, substantial identity work is often required for working-class students to 'fit in' after entering to elite institutions (Reay et al. 2010). This oftentimes leaves students caught in the middle of a transformative process, which 'renders working-class knowledge and experience deficient if not pathological' (Lehmann 2014: 13) and middle-class discourses not fully intelligible. These processes are at play even where students from lower SES backgrounds 'make it' to elite universities.

This sense of feeling like a 'fish out of water', feeling socially dislocated and excluded by institutional cultures and norms, is identified in many studies of working-class experience of higher education, in terms of engagement with higher education cultures (Read et al. 2003) at both newer and elite universities (e.g. Burke 2015; Finnegan and Merrill 2015). Those who research working-class drop-out also reveal a need to consider cultural narratives and the role of locality (e.g. Quinn et al. 2006). The weight of evidence, especially from the UK, is enormous. In Australia, more qualitative research into this phenomenon is desperately needed in terms of both how working-class young people negotiate this apparent mismatch between habitus and field and, relatedly, the issue of university attrition. This has recently come to fore, with Education Minister Simon Birmingham advancing that Higher Education Institutions should not take on students who will not complete their programs. Non-completion rates in Australia not only are high at over 1 in 4 but also exhibit a particularly classed and 'raced' profile. While as ever not being spoken of in class terms, low SES students make up 17% of enrolments but more than 31% of drop-outs (Moodie 2016). A class-based analysis is desperately needed. Drop out among indigenous students is more striking, with just over half dropping out, twice the national average. Integrating a Bourdieusian analysis would seem essential here to fully tackle both the class and 'raced' questions that emerge (taken up in Chapter 5).

Classed difference is also found in relation to the contemporary policy imperative to become employable and manage one's own prospective employability. Brooks and Everett (2009) distinguish how middle-class undergraduates from elite universities envisage their futures in very different ways to working-class students from 'lesser' institutions. Where working-class students made more active and anxiety-driven efforts to 'make things happen' for their careers, more privileged students expressed relative ease, being disinclined to form detailed plans for the future because, they felt, things 'would work out'. Furthermore, Wilton (2011) proffers that attending a newer, non-traditional, non-elite university appears to be a disadvantage for entry into top graduate positions, whether or not students demonstrate sufficient 'employability skills'.

Another significant driver of differentiated university experience has been whether or not young people (need to) pursue paid employment during their studies. Literature documenting the experiences of student employment attends to the issue in various ways, evaluating the prospect for skills acquisition and development, but also the implications of having a job upon educational attainment. We address this further in Chapter 4's discussion on youth, class and work, but in brief, those from marginalised social backgrounds are more likely to seek part-time employment and this risks exacerbating inequality (Moreau and Leathwood's 2006). This is confirmed in recent research by Roberts and Li (2016), which highlights the ways that even when social a cultural capital is unable to be translated into term time labour market success, middle-class students can deploy economic capital of their parents to cushion the blow of this joblessness, meaning that the quality of the diets, social activities or efforts at extra-curricular cultural enhancement are not sacrificed. The opposite was found for working-class students, whose lack of capital left them vulnerable to remaining lacking in access to many valuable capital building enterprises but also lacking the luxury to even contemplate that, for example the exam period should be a time when job searching can be allowed to become less of a priority. Middle-class students were willing and able to choose to avoid employment at times deemed detrimental for their studies.

Parental Use of Economic Capital

Within this discussion, we must also consider how parents and other family members play an important role in helping young people navigate the education and training system. Parents feel strong obligations to financially help and support their children when they go to university (Cobb-Clark and Gørgens 2014; Heath and Calvert 2013; West et al. 2015), but the level and type of support they might provide varies by social class practices and financial income. This has a significant impact on young people's experience of university. Evidence from the UK in the 1990s suggested that the average financial contribution made by parents to their child going to university was £300 a year, although major differences existed between classes. For example, those from social groups A and B made on average £1300 contribution per annum, while those from social groups D and E made only £50 (Callender and Kempson 1996). By 2011 these figures had jumped enormously.

Given the changing shift in how education was to be funded, moving from a public good to a private responsibility (France 2016), young people found themselves with higher costs, greater risk of debt and limited means to pay their own way (West et al. 2015). As a result, we start to see parents making greater contributions. For example, a national survey of UK student finances (Pollard et al. 2013) found that students who received most from families '...tended to be from more "traditional" student backgrounds: they were younger, white, living away from home, from managerial/professional backgrounds and single' (West et al. 2015: 26). The mean financial contribution from parents and other relatives to full-time students was £1603, although again class played a significant part in that those from professional or managerial backgrounds received a mean of £2310 and those from manual backgrounds £732 (Pollard et al. 2013). It was also the case that while 79% of students took a student loan, fewer students from managerial, professional or intermediate backgrounds took out maintenance loans than those from routine and manual backgrounds (Pollard et al. 2013). These trends are similar in Australia in that there has been a large increase in financial support given to students from parents. Again, the need for this arises due to the increased use of university fees and charges to students; parents in Australia feel under the same obligation and pressure to help all siblings (Cobb-Clark and Gørgens 2014).

Types of financial support could and does vary. For example, in qualitative research, West et al. (2015) showed how parents made contributions not only towards fees and accommodation costs but also towards everyday shopping, train fares, laptops, clothes and leisure items such as gym membership. This is sometimes further supplemented by grandparents and other family members. Australian research shows co-residence is a significant form of support. Most young people in Australia will attend a 'local' university and remain living in the family home, a major way of keeping costs of university low (Cobb-Clark and Gørgens 2014). That said, across both these studies class is a factor in that those from families with low incomes struggled to provide the same level of contribution as their middle-class counterparts. In Australia, those young people from families receiving welfare support are less likely to live at home as it brings an extra cost to the family that is hard to manage (Cobb-Clark and Gørgens 2014).

The level and type of resources young people receive has a major impact on the university experience. For example, West et al. (2015) show that young people who receive as gifts over 70% of their income to go to university have a lack of concern about money. They are able to make choices about whether they ought to find paid employment and the levels of debt they take on, while also enjoying university social life without too many concerns. They are also in a position to take on voluntary work or engage in strategies that enhance their CVs for the future job market. Alternatively, those who receive only 5% of their income from parents have increased levels of debt, find they have to work up to 20 hours a week and have to make trade-off between work and study. They feel more vulnerable and anxious about money and feel restricted in their ability to participate in university life or CV building (West et al. 2015).

Conclusion

Research, like that discussed earlier, has regularly documented that bridging 'socio-cultural incongruity' (Devlin 2013) is a necessity, but such findings have not led to an effective solution to class inequalities in post-compulsory education. One reason for class remaining a significant influence on outcomes and experiences in this wide range of ways, and something that is perhaps overlooked, is that education is a social field. Social fields are always sites of struggle over and about resources. As such they are subject to power struggles to shape or reshape the field. The widening of participation, in this sense, can be seen more as a token gesture, with the educational field remaining relatively intact, despite the changing nature of the population. The field remains intact *because* the dominant classes, those with a vested interest, resist changes that will act to their detriment or that will seemingly diminish 'their return'. Correspondingly, the 'rules of the game' remain relatively stable; this is the very business of social reproduction, offering an illusion of the prospects of social mobility but 'access without a reasonable chance of success is an empty phrase' (Devlin 2013: 940). Viewed this way, the research that determines repeatedly the incompatibility of individuals' habitus and various forms of capital with those of institutions is no real surprise. Even if we accept that students might be part of the 'joint venture' (Devlin 2013), to action such change and remedy the persistent inequities requires much more than efforts at ensuring that universities spell out their expectations for student involvement in learning. The arbitrary nature of what is classified as legitimate knowledge and culture needs to be fully exposed and revealed to be discriminatory. It is for this reason that social class must remain at the front of the research agenda and central to political discussion.

Notes

1. Though not without complications; see Gillborn 2010 for details.
2. In fact, after a downturn in 2012, UK student numbers bounced back strongly and increased in 2013 and 2014.
3. G08 universities are those (self) defined as the 'top', research intensive universities in Australia.

References

Allais, S. (2012). "Economics imperialism", education policy and educational theory. *Journal of Education Policy, 27*(2), 253–274.

Allen, K., & Hollingworth, S. (2013). 'Sticky subjects' or 'cosmopolitan creatives'? Social class, place and urban young people's aspirations for work in the knowledge economy. *Urban Studies, 50*(3), 499–517.

Ainley, P., & Allen, M. (2010). *Hard times for education in England.* London: Continuum Publishing.

Archer, L., Hutchings, M., & Ross, A. (2003). *Higher education and social class: Issues of exclusion and inclusion.* London: Routledge.

Archer, L., Hollingworth, S., & Halsall, A. (2007). University's not for me — I'm a Nike Person': Urban, working-class young people's negotiations of style', identity and educational engagement. *Sociology, 41*(2), 219–237.

Artess, J., McCulloch, A., & Mok, P. (2014). *Learning from Future track: studying and living at home.* BIS Research Paper No. 167. London: Department for Business Innovation and Skills.

Ball, S. J. (2003). *Class strategies and the education market place.* London: RoutledgeFalmer.

Ball, S. J., Davies, J., David, M., & Reay, D. (2002). 'Classification' and 'Judgement': Social class and the 'cognitive structures' of choice of higher education. *British Journal of Sociology of Education, 23*(1), 51–72.

Bates, I., & Riseborough, G. (1993). *Youth and inequality.* Milton Keynes: Open University Press.

Bathmaker, A. M., Ingram, N., & Waller, R. (2013). Higher education, social class and the mobilisation of capitals: Recognising and playing the game. *British Journal of Sociology of Education, 34*(5–6), 723–743.

Berrington, A., Roberts, S., & Tammes, P. (2016). Educational aspirations among UK young teenagers: Exploring the role of gender, class and ethnicity. *British Educational Research Journal, 42*(5), 729–755.

BIS. (2015). *Widening Participation in Higher Education,* London: Department for Business Innovation and Skills, https://www.gov.uk/government/uploads/system/uploads/attachment_data/file/443986/Widen-Partic-HE-2015s.pdf.

Bok, J. (2010). The capacity to aspire to higher education: 'It's like making them do a play without a script'. *Critical Studies in Education, 51*(2), 163–178.

Boliver, V. (2013). How fair is access to more prestigious UK universities?. *The British Journal of Sociology, 64*(2), 344–364.

Bourdieu, P. (1973). The three forms of theoretical knowledge. *Social Science Information, 12*(1), 53–80.

Bradley, D., Noonan, P., Nugent, H., & Scales, B. (2008). *Review of Australian higher education: Final report.* (Bradley review), Canberra: Department of Education, Employment and Workplace Relations.

Bradley, H., & Ingram, N. (2013). Banking on the future: Choices, aspirations and economic hardship in working-class student experience. In Atkinson, W., Roberts, S., Savage, M. (eds.), *Class inequality in austerity Britain* (pp. 51–69). Basingstoke: Palgrave Macmillan.

Brine, J. (2006). Lifelong learning and the knowledge economy: Those that know and those that do not—the discourse of the European Union. *British Educational Research Journal, 32*(5), 649–665.

Brooks, R., & Everett, G. (2009). Post-graduation reflections on the value of a degree. *British Educational Research Journal, 35*(3), 333–349.

Brown, P. (2013). Education, opportunity and the prospects for social mobility. *British Journal of Sociology of Education, 34*(5), 678–699.

Brown, P., Lauder, H., & Ashton, D. (2011). *The global auction: The broken promises of education, jobs, and incomes.* Oxford: Oxford University Press.

Burke, C. (2015). *Culture, capitals and graduate futures: Degrees of class.* London: Routledge.

Callender, C., & Kempson, E. (1996). *Student finances: Income, expenditure and take-up of student loans.* London: Policy Studies Institute.

Campbell, C., Proctor, H., & Sherington, G. (2009). *School choice: How parents negotiate the new school market in Australia.* Crows Nest NSW: Allen and Unwin.

Chesters, J., & Watson, L. (2013). Understanding the persistence of inequality in higher education: Evidence from Australia. *Journal of Education Policy, 28*(2), 198–215.

Clark, D. (2002). *Participation in post compulsory education in England: What explains the boom and bust?* London: Centre for the Economics of Education, London School of Economics and Political Science.

Cobb-Clark, D. A., & Gørgens, T. (2014). Parents' economic support of young-adult children: Do socioeconomic circumstances matter? *Journal of Population Economics, 27*(2), 447–471.

Coffield, F. (1999). Breaking the consensus: Lifelong learning as social control. *British Educational Research Journal, 25*(4), 479–499.

Crawford, C., & Greaves, E. (2015). *Socio-economic, ethnic and gender differences in HE participation*, BIS Research Paper No. 186. London: Department for Business Innovation and Skills.

Crozier, G., & Reay, D. (2011). Capital accumulation: Working-class students learning how to learn in higher education. *Teaching in Higher Education*, *16*(2), 145–155.

Crozier, G., Reay, D., Clayton, J., Colliander, L., & Grinstead, J. (2008). Different strokes for different folks: Diverse students in diverse institutions–experiences of higher education. *Research Papers in Education*, *23*(2), 167–177.

Devlin, M. (2013). Bridging socio-cultural incongruity: Conceptualising the success of students from low socio-economic status backgrounds in Australian higher education. *Studies in Higher Education*, *38*(6), 939–949.

DfEE. (1998). *Higher education in the 21st century*. Sheffield: Department of Education and Employment.

Donnelly, M. (2015). A new approach to researching school effects on higher education participation. *British Journal of Sociology of Education*, *36*(7), 1073–1090.

Edwards, D., & McMillan, J. (2015). Completing university in Australia: A cohort analysis exploring equity group outcomes. *Joining the dots: research briefing*, May 2015, Australian Council for Educational Research.

Eikhof, D., & Warhurst, C. (2013). The promised land? Why social inequalities are systemic in the creative industries. *Employee Relations*, *35*(5), 495–508.

Evans, S. (2009). In a different place: Working-class girls and higher education. *Sociology*, *43*(2), 340–355.

Feng, H., & Lu, M. (2013). School quality and housing prices: Empirical evidence from a natural experiment in Shanghai, China. *Journal of Housing Economics*, *22*(4), 291–307.

Finnegan, F., & Merrill, B. (2015). 'We're as good as anybody else': A comparative study of working-class university students' experiences in England and Ireland. *British Journal of Sociology of Education*, 1–18.

Forsyth, A., & Furlong, A. (2000). *Socioeconomic disadvantage and access to higher education*. York: Joseph Rowntree Foundation.

France, A. (2016). *Understanding youth in the global economic crisis*. Bristol: Policy Press.

France, A., & Roberts, S. (2015). The problem of social generations: A critique of the new emerging orthodoxy in youth studies. *Journal of Youth Studies*, *18*(2), 215–230.

Gale, T., & Tranter, D. (2011). Social justice in Australian higher education policy: An historical and conceptual account of student participation. *Critical studies in education*, *52*(1), 29–46.

Gibbons, S. (2012) *The link between schools and house prices is now an established fact*, LSE Blogs, http://eprints.lse.ac.uk/48622/1/blogs.lse.ac.uk-The_link_ between_schools_and_house_prices_is_now_an_established_fact.pdf.

Gillborn, D. (2010). The white working class, racism and respectability: Victims, degenerates and interest-convergence. *British Journal of Educational Studies*, 58(1), 3–25.

Goldthorpe, J. H., & Jackson, M. (2007). Intergenerational class mobility in contemporary Britain: political concerns and empirical findings. *The British journal of sociology*, 58(4), 525–546.

Goos, M., & Manning, A. (2007). Lousy and lovely jobs: The rising polarization of work in Britain. *The review of economics and statistics*, 89(1), 118–133.

Gore, J., Holmes, K., Smith, M., Southgate, E., & Albright, J. (2015). Socioeconomic status and the career aspirations of Australian school students: Testing enduring assumptions. *The Australian Educational Researcher*, 42(2), 155–177.

Green, F., & Zhu, Y. (2010). Over qualification, job dissatisfaction, and increasing dispersion in the returns to graduate education. *Oxford Economic Papers*, 62(4), 740–763.

Grey, S., & Scott, J. (2012). When the government steers the market: Implications for the New Zealand tertiary education system. In *Future of Higher Education Conference, University of Sydney*.

Hansen, K. (2014). Moving house for education in the pre-school years. *British Educational Research Journal*, 40(3), 483–500.

Heath, S., & Calvert, E. (2013). Gifts, loans and intergenerational support for young adults. *Sociology*, 47(6), 1120–1135.

Hodkinson, P. (1998). How young people make career decisions. *Education+training*, 40(6), 301–306.

Holloway, S. L., & Pimlott-Wilson, H. (2011). The politics of aspiration: neoliberal education policy, 'low' parental aspirations, and primary school extended services in disadvantaged communities. *Children's Geographies*, 9(1), 79–94.

Howells, K. (1997) Address by Mr Kim Howells - Minister of lifelong learning, UK, UNESCO Fifth International Conference on Adult Education, Hamburg, 24-28 July 1997. http://www.unesco.org/education/uie/confintea/pdf/fin repeng.pdf.

Johnson, C. (2004). Mark Latham and the ideology of the ALP. *Australian Journal of Political Science*, 39, 535–552.

Keane, E. (2011). Distancing to self-protect: The perpetuation of inequality in higher education through socio-relational dis/engagement. *British Journal of Sociology of Education*, 32(3), 449–466.

Keep, E., & Mayhew, K. (2010). Moving beyond skills as a social and economic panacea. *Work, Employment and Society*, 24(3), 565–577.

Kenway, J. (2013). Challenging inequality in Australian schools: Gonski and beyond. *Discourse: Studies in the Cultural Politics of Education, 34*(2), 286–308.
Koh, A., & Kenway, J. (2016). *Elite schools: Multiple geographies of privilege.* London: Routledge.
Lawton, K. (2009). *Nice work if you can get it.* London: Institute for Public Policy Research.
Lehmann, W. (2012). Extra-credential experiences and social closure: Working-class students at university. *British Educational Research Journal, 38,* 203–218.
Lehmann, W. (2014). Habitus transformation and hidden injuries: Successful working-class university students. *Sociology of Education, 87*(1), 1–15.
Machin, S., & Salvanes, K. G. (2016). Valuing school quality via a school choice reform. *The Scandinavian Journal of Economics, 118*(1), 3–24.
Mizen, P. (2004). *The changing state of youth.* Basingstoke: Palgrave.
Moodie, G. (2016) Which students are most likely to drop out of university, *The Conversation,* https://theconversation.com/which-students-are-most-likely-to-drop-out-of-university-56276
Moreau, M. P., & Leathwood, C. (2006). Graduates' employment and the discourse of employability: A critical analysis. *Journal of Education and Work, 19*(4), 305–324.
Morrison, A. (2014). Hegemony through responsibilisation: Getting working-class students into higher education in the United Kingdom. *Power and Education,* 6(2), 118–129.
Mullen, A. L. (2009). Elite destinations: Pathways to attending an Ivy League university. *British Journal of Sociology of Education, 30*(1), 15–27.
Norton, A. (2015). *Mapping Australia higher education 2014–15.* Australia, Grattan Institute: Carlton Victoria.
OECD. (1996). The knowledge based economy, Paper no. OCDE/GD (96)102, OECD Publishing, https://www.oecd.org/sti/sci-tech/1913021.pdf.
OECD. (2013) Education at a Glance 2013, OECD Indicators, OECD Publishing, https://www.oecd.org/edu/eag2013%20(eng)–FINAL%2020%20June%202013.pdf.
Papapolydorou, M. (2014). 'When you see a normal person...' social class and friendship networks among teenage students. *British Journal of Sociology of Education, 35*(4), 559–577.
Parry, G., Callender, C., Temple, P., & Scott, P. (2012). *Understanding higher education in further education colleges,* BIS Research Paper no. 69. London: Department for Business Innovation and Skills.
Peacock, D., Sellar, S., & Lingard, B. (2014). The activation, appropriation and practices of student-equity policy in Australian higher education. *Journal of Education Policy, 29*(3), 377–396.

Pollard, E., Hunt, W., Hillage, J., Drever, E., Chanfreau, J., & Coutinho, S. (2013). *Student income and expenditure survey 2012*, BIS Research Paper no. 115. London: Department for Business Innovation and Skills.

Purcell, K.,., Elias, P., Atfield, G., Behle, H., Ellison, R., & Luchinskaya, D. (2013) Transitions into employment, further study and other outcomes, The Future track stage 4 Report, *Manchester/Coventry: HECSU/Warwick Institute for Employment Research*.

Quinn, J., Thomas, L., Slack, K., Casey, L., Thexton, W., & Noble, J. (2006). Lifting the hood: Lifelong learning and young, white, provincial working-class masculinities. *British Educational Research Journal*, 32(5), 735–750.

Raco, M. (2009). From expectations to aspirations: State modernisation, urban policy, and the existential politics of welfare in the UK. *Political Geography*, 28(7), 436–444.

Read, B., Archer, L., & Leathwood, C. (2003). Challenging cultures? Student conceptions of 'belonging' and 'isolation' at a post-1992 university. *Studies in Higher Education*, 28(3), 261–277.

Reay, D., & Ball, S. J. (1998). 'Making their Minds Up': Family dynamics of school choice. *British Educational Research Journal*, 24(4), 431–448.

Reay, D., Crozier, G., & J. Clayton. (2010). "Fitting in" or "standing out': Working-class students in UK higher education. *British Educational Research Journal*, 32(1), 1–19.

Reay, D., David, M. E., & Ball, S. J. (2005). *Degrees of choice: Class, race, gender and higher education*. London: Trentham Books.

Roberts, K. (1995). *Youth and employment in modern Britain*. Oxford: Oxford University.

Roberts, S., & Evans, S. (2013). 'Aspirations' and imagined futures: The im/possibilities for Britain's young working class. In *Class inequality in austerity Britain* (pp. 70–89). Palgrave Macmillan UK.

Roberts, S., & Li, Z. (2016). Capital limits: Social class, motivations for term-time job searching and the consequences of joblessness among UK university students. *Journal of Youth Studies*, 1–18.

Savage, M. (2000). *Class analysis and social transformation*. Buckingham: Open University Press.

Savage, M. (2015). *Social class in the 21st century*. Penguin UK.

Sellar, S., Gale, T., & Parker, S. (2011). Appreciating aspirations in Australian higher education. *Cambridge Journal of Education*, 41(1), 37–52.

Skeggs, B. (1997). *Formations of class and gender*. London: Sage.

Smyth, E., & Banks, J. (2012). 'There was never really any question of anything else': Young people's agency institutional habitus and the transition to higher education. *British Journal of Sociology of Education*, 33(2), 263–281.

Social Mobility and Poverty Commission. (2013). *Higher education: The fair access challenge*. London: Social Mobility and Poverty Commission.

St Clair, R., & Benjamin, A. (2013). Performing desires: The dilemma of aspirations and educational attainment. *British Educational Research Journal, 37*(3), 501–517.

Stahl, G. (2015). *Identity, Neoliberalism and Aspiration: Educating white working-class boys*. London: Routledge.

Strand, S. (2014). Ethnicity, gender, social class and achievement gaps at age 16: Intersectionality and 'Getting it' for the white working class. *Research Papers in Education, 29*(2), 131–171.

Strathdee, R., & Engler, R. (2012). Who is missing from higher education in New Zealand? *British Educational Research Journal, 38*(3), 497–514.

Tomlinson, S. (2013). *Ignorant yobs? Low attainers in a global knowledge economy*. London: Routledge.

West, A., Roberts, J., Lewis, J., & Noden, P. (2015). Paying for higher education in England: Funding policy and families. *British Journal of Educational Studies, 63*(1), 23–45.

Wheelahan, L. (2008). Neither fish nor fowl: The contradiction at the heart of Australian tertiary education. *Journal of Access Policy and Practice, 5*(2), 133–152.

Whitty, G., & Edwards, T. (1998). School choice policies in England and the United States: An exploration of their origins and significance. *Comparative Education, 34*(2), 211–227.

Willis, P. E. (1977). *Learning to labor: How working class kids get working class jobs*. Farnborough: Saxon House.

Wilton, N. (2011). Do employability skills really matter in the UK graduate labour market? The case of business and management graduates. *Work, Employment and Society, 25*(1), 85–100.

CHAPTER 4

Young People, Work and Social Class

Abstract Historically, employment has featured significantly in how class has been theorised and understood in youth sociology. In contemporary debates about the changing nature of work for young people, the impact of these changes on different classes has been marginalised. While developments such as underemployment, unemployment and precariousness are real and significant, we suggest they must be analysed through a class lens. In this context, academic work inspired and influenced by Pierre Bourdieu can help illuminate both the dynamic and embedded nature of class relationships in young people's experience of work.

Keywords Class · Youth · Employment · Aspirations · Poor work · Graduate employment

SOCIAL CLASS IN STUDIES OF YOUNG PEOPLE'S WORKING LIVES: AN ISSUE OF DIMINISHING INTEREST

Given youth research's interest in the education-work nexus, and especially school-to-work transitions, social class long held a pivotal place in analyses of structural constraints on young people's origins and destinations (Pollock 2008). This is well exemplified by Carter's (1962) classic text *Home, School and Work*, where the influence of social class on these domains feels sown into the very fabric of the book. This is also the case for other key studies on school-to-work transitions from

© The Author(s) 2017
A. France, S. Roberts, *Youth and Social Class*,
DOI 10.1057/978-1-137-57829-7_4

69

the UK, like the seminal works of Roberts (1968) and Ashton and Field (1976). In the former, Roberts developed a theory of transitional outcomes that deviated from ideas of 'occupational choice' towards understandings based on 'opportunity structure'. For the latter, Ashton and Field were able to explain how a complex amalgam of experiences at home and school intertwined with social class to produce a relatively narrow set of career alternatives. Class background, here, formed part of the *predictive* element of their theory of a tripartite outcomes typology: careerless, short-term and extended careers. This theme was similarly taken up in Willis' (1977) classic text, which documented the processes through which working-class kids are readied in education, and are themselves complicit for ending up in working-class jobs. Beyond the 'core' of the sub-discipline of youth studies, work and youth were important subjects, with generalists like Norbert Elias, one of the great sociologists of the twentieth century, for example, having researched young people's integration into employment and workplace socialisation in ways that paid significant (if not always entirely ethical) attention to social class in the 1960s (Goodwin and O'Connor 2016). Yet, as we shall show, emphasis on the relationship between class and young people's work has been diminishing.

Since the late 1970s, a changing employment landscape in most industrialised nations formed one part of a two-pronged problem for the sociology of youth in respect of work and class analysis. Relatively predictable labour market outcomes were increasingly undermined by neoliberal flexible work practices, growths in non-standard forms of employment and significant restructuring of economies as manufacturing and heavy industry was significantly outsourced. A growing service sector would come to dominate most economies in the proceeding decades. High levels of youth unemployment but also, as a policy response, an array of expanding pathways into education followed (see Chapter 3). The subsequent policy imperative of widening educational participation and its associated 'enterprise culture' (MacDonald and Coffield, 1990) of encouraging young people into youth training schemes meant that young people were often artificially 'warehoused' (Roberts 1995), remaining outside of the unemployment statistics and seemingly developing their human capital to make them more job ready. Most importantly, the focus on youth, class and transitions to employment became diluted; in part because of the huge number of young people who were not in work, and at a time when they were not necessarily expected to be. In the UK, for example, 16 year olds entering work fell from 62% of the cohort in 1975 to just 9% in 1992 (Maguire and Maguire 1999).

The second part of this two-pronged problem for class analysis in the sociology of youth was the cultural turn and the rise of identity politics. Despite this turn towards the 'cultural' in sociology, studies of transitions were still documenting origins and destinations of young people for at least 15 years (see Bates and Riseborough 1993). These interests were explored across borders with studies such as Dwyer et al. (1984) in Australia following a cultural class analysis of training schemes and young people's movement into work. However, with the political New Right's strategic de-emphasising of social class in all public and political discourses, a widespread societal retreat from the language of class during the 1980s – captured by Thatcher's infamous argument that class was an unhelpful, communist concept that set people against one another (see Cannadine 2000) – meant that such studies were lacking in outright emphasis on social class that was the hallmark of previous decades. Transitions approaches also received sharp criticisms, with the 'counting up' of transitions positioned as descriptive, dry and theoretically empty (Miles 2000).

During this period the role of class had become complicated, with some empirical studies, for example, drawing out the significance of the intersection of class with locality as an important axis of inequality. Ashton and Maguire (1986), for instance, showed how working-class men living closer to London were less likely to suffer unemployment than middle-class men from the North of England (see also MacDonald and Coffield 1990). However, in a policy environment that had moved further and further away from structural explanations of youth unemployment towards individualised explanations, focus began to fall on what was described as 'the underclass thesis'. Proposed by US conservative commentator Charles Murray (1990), this thesis proposed that welfare state dependency had created a 'dangerous class', epitomised by anti-social and anti-work attitudes and culturally set apart from the majority of mainstream, work-motivated society. Such ideas held substantial traction in countries such as the UK, Australia and New Zealand (Humpage 2016) especially within policy realms and in the public imagination. For the most part, at first at least, these were not well tackled or dismissed (see MacDonald 1999). MacDonald (1999; et al. 2001; with Marsh, 2005 and with Shildrick and Furlong 2014) has since done more than most to tackle the underclass thesis, repeatedly demonstrating strong desires for work amongst those who comprise this alleged underclass, and challenging the myth of worklessness and benefit dependency. However, these are notions that persist powerfully in the public imagination. This happens because, in the current climate of enhanced state retrenchment, austerity is often justified by policymakers by reference to this welfare-reliant, work-shy 'other' in the UK through language such as the divide between 'workers' and 'shirkers', and in Australia and New Zealand through the rhetoric of the 'dole bludger'. Indeed, late 2016 OECD data showing large increases since the Global financial crisis (GFC) in the number of young Australians who were not in education, employment or training (NEET) was widely framed in the media as an issue of welfare dependency and laziness. *The Daily Telegraph*, for example, talked explicitly about NEETs as 'the new dole bludger'.

With the emergence of 'third way' politics in UK, Australia and New Zealand in the 1990s, talk of class – 'under' or otherwise – in labour market discussions was jettisoned in favour of a focus on 'social exclusion'. While widely deemed to be more palatable than the language of the underclass, for us this may have come to be a clever sleight of phrase that enabled the language of poverty to remain out of public discourse (Levitas 2005) and limited discussion of wealth distribution (Matheison et al. 2008). This new language, which still emphasised the problems faced by *individuals* (not classes), was accompanied by growing sociological focus on 'voice' and subjectivities. Simultaneously, despite being a long-standing concern for youth sociologists, employment issues became the poor relation in research terms. As a legacy, for example, between 2011 and 2015 young people's experiences of employment and unemployment account for just about a tenth of articles in the *Journal of Youth Studies*, and fewer still take into consideration a broader body of actors or stakeholders in the wider political economy of youth (Sukarieh and Tannock 2016). We find this problematic and as a weakness in current youth scholarship.

How Youth Became the Central Dimension of Inequality: A Development of an Unhelpful Mischaracterisation

Where a focus on youth and employment remains it has often been done so in ways that cast youth and young people in a relatively homogenous fashion. There are, perhaps, understandable reasons for this. Young people are more likely to be unemployed and underemployed (i.e. working less hours than desired or needed) – a trend that is amplified during economic recessions, with the recent GFC being no different (France 2016). Also, they are subject to a range of other detrimental experiences. For example, young people are more likely to experience non-payment, especially for attending meetings or training; to be underpaid; to miss out on meal breaks; to work illegally long shifts; to feel pressured to work overtime and, as has been the case for decades, to have higher chances of workplace injury (Furlong et al. 2017). Youth wages, the *institutionalised* process of paying young people lesser rates than their adult counter parts, are multi-layered and widely practiced and formally noted in minimum wage legislations (France 2016).

This reminds us that youth is in itself a site of inequality (France 2016). Yet, it is the advent of recent economic changes that has led to calls that we ought to understand the contemporary youth period as being a distinctive new social generation (Woodman and Wyn 2015). This change is argued to require new sociological concepts and a prioritisation of young people's subjectivities to understand youth's present condition. From a more materialist perspective, Cote also points to recently occurring '...systemic proletarianisation of the entire youth population in many countries' (2014: 527), leading to calls for a recognition of youth-as-class. As will become clear, our position deviates from both these accounts and we contend that making class analyses central will foster greater understanding. For the moment, though, it is worth taking some time to outline some changes used to underpin the previous claims.

Labour market changes, despite slightly differing chronologies, are products of globalisation and are trends that have resonated across advanced economies, especially the Anglo-economies (France 2016). Paid employment, indeed, has undergone one of the most remarkable and significant changes in the post-war period (McDowell 2012). The golden age of youth employment in the post-war period may not have been unproblematic for everyone (Vickerstaff 2003), but this period did exhibit a few core predictabilities. Adult wages, for instance, were easier to achieve as a young person (though not for apprentices), with a relative plenty of unskilled work offering jobs and wages commensurate with or even beyond what one might earn in white collar jobs. Holding no qualifications was not necessarily a significant hindrance to getting certain kinds of work, right up until the late 1970s (Furlong et al. 2017). The industrialised era of work gave way to the 'post-fordist' economy, with its associated flexible labour market practices being the hall mark of a newly unleashed neo-liberal approach to governance. This has returned fewer jobs for young people and/or dragged down youth wages; indeed, increasing numbers of non-standard forms of employment, and also part-time work, has corresponded with greater declines in relative youth wages in Australia, New Zealand, the UK and other 'advanced' nations (France 2016; Furlong et al. 2017). Non-standard forms of employment, we should note, are associated with disproportionately higher rates of poverty in advanced and developing economies compared to permanent full-time formal employee arrangements.[1] Despite having youth-wide implications, managing these structural changes and associated challenges is contingent on access to family and class-based social, economic and cultural capital to cushion these difficult new realities, as we address in the following.

Of these new forms of employment, the rise of zero hours contracts and also increased numbers of independent contractors (i.e. self-employed) working in the collaborative economy have particular interest for the study of young people, for both are strongly present in the kinds of low level, front line service jobs where young people are overly represented. Both are positioned by industry bosses as being important developments in offering flexibility, allowing workers to fit the job around existing commitments, but such jobs lack wage and contract protections. The most prominent recent example of such practices is the meals delivery firm 'deliveroo', where, being independent contractors rather than employees, work is paid at piece rate: in Australia, at the time of writing, for new workers this is AUS$0 per hour but AUS$10 per delivery. During times of peak demand this can be relatively attractive, but disputes between workers and bosses in several international cities in mid-2016 highlight how such work can pay very little when there is scare work to go around large numbers of people. This on the one hand might seem like genuine, small-scale entrepreneurship, but might be better conceived of as a 'bogus form of self-employment' (Furlong et al. 2017); the epitome of what is sometimes called 'the gig economy' (Friedman 2014).

As temporary positions become more common and organisations progressively turn to contracting independent workers for short-term engagements, an economy becomes increasingly dominated by precarious work, uncertainty and unpredictability from the point of view of the worker (Kalleberg 2009: 2). Following a long-standing trend, market risks have increasingly been transferred to workers and away from firms. The changes outlined earlier might in some ways represent more obviously concerning trends, and there is no question that governments of Australia, UK and New Zealand are actively positioning self-employment and entrepreneurship as solutions to youth unemployment (France 2016). However, young people in advanced nations comprise very small proportions of independent contractors. In 2013, for instance, the under 25s formed just 4.7% of all independent contractors in the Australia (ABS 2016), and just 5% of UK independent contractors in 2014 (Jones et al. 2015). The wider and clear majority experience of work among young people, then, is in the form of an employment relationship – but such relationships do not obviate the prospect of a precarious existence.

Economists have recently noted that there has been increasing job polarisation (Autor 2010) between 'lousy' and 'lovely' jobs (Goos et al. 2010), and an attendant hollowing out of the middle segment of industrialised economies as moderately skilled manual labour has been replaced by technology. This trend has increased in the aftermath of the GFC (Jaimovich and Siu 2012). Despite the nationally variant effects of the GFC (e.g. Australia fared *relatively* better than UK and New Zealand),[2] young people are disproportionately likely to do the kinds roles that fall into the lousy side of this dichotomy: jobs returning not just short, fixed or zero hours contracts, but low and falling relative rates of pay and high levels of insecurity. Indeed, young people in Australia, UK and New Zealand and well beyond, from the USA to Japan and in many parts of Europe, are often targeted specifically by restaurants and retailers to take on jobs with such conditions because, being more likely to live at the parental home and/or remaining on the extended path through education, they are more amenable to low wages and part time, evening or weekend work (Sukarieh and Tannock 2015). It is no wonder then that Standing, famous for his assessment that such conditions give rise to the emergence of a 'new class', explains that while anyone can fall into this 'precariat', 'the most common image is of young people emerging from school and college to enter a precarious existence lasting years' (Standing 2011: 65).

Ultimately, for all the focus in research and policy texts on youth as consumers, young people remain an important and significant part of the workforce (Sukarieh and Tannock 2015). It also seems clear that as Gallie and Paugam suggest that 'employment does not guarantee social integration: in the longer run, poor quality jobs are likely to make many people highly vulnerable to job loss and to eventual labour market marginalisation' (2002: 62). This seems to be of particular pertinence during the youth period, when experiences tend to solidify social disadvantage and shape future patterns in respect of housing and domestic transitions.

These developments are very real. It is not our intention to get bogged down in debates about the absolute novelty of the 'new' conditions or the extent to which the corresponding experiences represent a historical first. In short, we sit with those who argue that precarity has deep roots and has long existed in various forms (Skeggs 2004; Furlong et al. 2017). Our major concern is to raise caution and intervene in what has become the relative marginalisation of social class analysis in youth sociology. While enjoying something of a renaissance in wider social research, how class resources are utilised by young people to navigate these new conditions appears secondary to a concentration on the changed social and economic landscape in and of itself.

It is not necessarily the intention of youth scholars to abandon the idea of social class as a dimension of difference; however, commonalities of experience that cut across the social hierarchy appear to be brought to the fore, and in doing so class analysis becomes side stepped. For example, Furlong et al. (2011: 363) highlight that '...ability to navigate uncertainty and drive, resourcefulness and life-management skills' are key features of young people's engagement with contemporary labour markets. More tellingly in the parentheses after this they note '...which are not necessarily class-based resources.' Our reading of this situation would be that it ought to be the other way round, with the critical and most powerful feature of these processes being that class-based resources can and are mobilised to protect and advance one's interests. A better parenthesised note would have been that 'other traits', such as those described, might also be part of the analysis. Even then, we would insist upon considering the relationship between class resources and the development of 'drive' and 'life management skills' to avoid reliance on individualistic, trait-theory style explanations. We also have reservations about the way they discuss 'on-call' employment as a feature of all spheres of life, for both casual service workers and also young knowledge workers.

This extends to Woodman's (2012) very useful identification of shifting temporal structures as an axis of inequality. Here, we suggest much more thorough attendance to how this process is coloured by class background would have richer and more meaningful impact upon revealing and alleviating inequalities. Our chief concern, again, is youth itself becomes the dimension of inequality most revered. This is vibrantly illustrated in Sukarieh and Tannock's (2015) recent book, where they 'doth their cap' to James Cote's (2014) position that inequality by age or life stage is pivotal; their counter critique ends up sounding more like a string of praise, followed by an all-important but yet again parenthesised sentence: '(social and economic inequalities among youth and among adults are probably far greater than inequalities between the two groups as a whole)' (Sukarieh and Tannock 2015: 136). Class inequality is the bigger story and should not be relegated to single sentences in parentheses.

An Unapologetic Emphasis on How Social Class Shapes Young People's Experiences of Employment

The contemporary youth period should not be characterised by broad and largely all-encompassing modal patterns. This chapter is now used to illustrate how social class matters in substantive and meaningful ways in a variety of employment type engagements. Before we build this argument through the extant literature, we also want to note that while arguments for moving away from analyses of class difference are sometimes part of a holistic critique of the continuing relevance and appropriateness of analytical tools (e.g. Wyn and Woodman's 2006 argument for 'generational' analysis in youth studies), some have argued that unclear evidence of social class implications requires *better but still class related concepts*. For example, Muntaner et al. (2010) explain that when small employers can exhibit worse health than highly skilled workers, and supervisors can display worse health than frontline workers, the necessary response is to develop *new social class concepts* and measures to explain social inequalities. This is similar for Chesters et al. (2007) who, after finding increasing diversity among workers classified as being in 'own account/self-employed', called for greater attention to be paid to education and occupation levels. This approach rejected the idea that class was not relevant in discussion of such workers despite the fact that they were no longer an obvious, unitary social group.

What we want to foreground here is that social and economic change is not something that leaves our approaches stymied. Changes in the economy such as those outlined before do not make it impossible or even especially difficult to analyse youth's contemporary condition from a class perspective. In fact, Bourdieu's theoretical tools lend themselves to an analysis of changes in the economy that we have highlighted in the earlier passages. Central to Bourdieu's field theory is an understanding that social environments are dynamic, complex and made up of interacting and unequal forces, that is fields are 'historical constellations that arise, grow, change shape, and sometimes wane or perish, over time' (Wacquant 2007: 268). The battle for resources that takes place within them, thus, remains an important area of interest *despite and because* of the changes to the field. Youth studies concerns the effects of broader economic and labour market change and, most crucially, identifying which groups have been most affected and why, and also how they suffer and how they cope (Roberts 1995: 23). And this is what we attempt now in the remainder of the chapter.

WORKING DURING EDUCATION

Before a discussion about employment destinations and graduate experiences of work, it is important to recognise that one major change in relation to work is the evolution of student employment. As before, the 1980s youth unemployment rates and, in tandem, social policy aimed at extending the educational transition ensured paid work was not normatively expected for young people. However, the continuation of these educational reforms, such as expansion of the university sector, but especially its marketisation, has led to larger than ever numbers of young people engaging in higher education (Jewell 2014). The distinction between work and education has become blurred, and the two fields now exhibit some intimate overlaps; as the numbers of young people in university has grown, so too has the proportion of students who combine work (most often part-time) and study. For UK students this figure is over 50%, and this is similar in Australia and New Zealand. Tuition fees, through first their introduction, and then various and quite dramatic hikes are one part of the explanation, yet increased fees are only part of the story. There has been a steady abolition of state maintenance grants, and while they have been replaced with loans and a wide range of bursaries (France 2016), the cost of being a student requires more than this fee payments: rent, bills, food and drink, costs for books, materials and/or extracurricular activities, travel, clothing, socialising and so on (France 2016). In short, students have significant living costs, like everyone else. Simultaneously, the student worker is the idealised employee for a service sector economy that promotes flexibility, transience and limited commitment as necessities for business competitiveness and idealised virtues for staff. While quantitative studies of the phenomenon reveal that meeting financial needs appear to be a primary concern, it should be noted that students, of course, take up work also to enhance employability (Jewell 2014; Roberts and Li 2016).

Some research presents part-time work as a largely beneficial experience for under graduates. Skills relevant for future careers, as well as confidence and other abilities advantageous for studies and in-class contributions sometimes outweigh students' observations that employment lowers lecture attendance rates (see Curtis and Shani 2002; Martin and McCabe 2007). However, Callender's (2008) thorough multi-subject, multi-institutional research in the UK seems rather telling. Callender confirms that term-time working detrimentally affects final-year marks and degree results, with a stark and simple correlation: the more hours students work, the less likely they are to obtain a good degree. Given lower social class students are more likely to seek part-time employment, such employment risks exacerbating inequality. This is supported by recent statistical analyses undertaken by Jewell (2014), whose sophisticated statistical analysis demonstrates that term-time employment is more likely to be undertaken for financial reasons than for enhancement of transferrable skills, and that people with such motivations are more likely to be 'from lower socioeconomic backgrounds, had less financial support from their families and had therefore a higher expected debt on graduation' (2014: 10). Tellingly, she explains the *advantages of not having to work*, stating unequivocally that 'those who are obliged to work, or who work with a greater intensity [...] experience the larger negative effects on their academic performance' (see also Roberts and Li 2016). Some research points out complexities, such as how working-class students present their jobs as opportunities to build a sense of belonging or even leadership skills (Satterlee 2009), but ultimately results in them being less likely to engage in valuable extra curricula activity (Satterlee 2009; Bathmaker et al. 2013; also see Chapter 3). These patterns of inequality are reflected in recent data from New Zealand, where Richardson et al.'s (2013) show the number of hours worked directly negatively effects grades of employed students. It's not employment during studies per se that are problematic, but the *need* to work and the amount of time committed that is of issue – and motivations to work longer are very often associated with needing to finance pressures; they are classed pressures. The effect employment has upon studies at younger ages is also noteworthy. While jobs during compulsory schooling sometimes facilitate becoming employed full-time upon school completion, this might be seen as expediting post-compulsory drop out (Patton and Smith 2009). Furthermore, Rokicka (2014) analysis of the UK's LYPSE data shows that part-time employment undertaken in the final year of compulsory education is detrimental to academic outcomes and to participation in education in the subsequent year, echoing Vickers and colleagues' (2003) findings in relation to Australia's LSAY data. Related to this are conceptions of and aspirations for career (see also discussion in Chapter 3 on aspirations for education).

CLASSED ASPIRATIONS FOR WORK

Young people are often thought to have internalised the neo-liberal policy emphasis on individualism, reflexivity and agency in relation to career choices (Brannen and Nilsen 2002; McDonald et al. 2011), but even here there are class differences even to consider. Recent research has challenged the dominant narrative that middle-class young people are the idealised contemporary reflexive subject. For example, Laughland-Booÿ et al.'s (2015) interviews with 16–17-year-old Australians show that privileged social locations produce a sense of security from various social risks. It correspondingly produces a non-reflexive perspective that leads to career choices based on social norms rather than a sense of their ability. This is echoed in the UK, with Brooks and Everett (2009) highlighting how middle-class young people hold a confident attitude that 'it'll all work out' in terms of labour market outcomes, while working-class students more often expect to *actively* negotiate their future employment trajectories. Similar finding emerges from the work of Borlagdan (2015), who reports that active negotiation and the anticipation of managing risks is often the preserve of Australian young people from low SES backgrounds. More well-resourced (middle class) young people are able to mobilise capitals to better cope with periods or uncertainty in their transition (Borlagdan 2015; Roberts and Li 2016). This perspective echoes Atkinson's (2013) findings in relation to the wider adult working population's understanding of the prospect of unemployment or redundancy. Here, ability to project forward to future, or alternatively remain focussed on the present and/or remain cynical about the future, was stratified by class position in the social space.

These perspectives on understandings of the future have varying implications for working-class youth. Roberts and Evans (2013) show what might be described as 'modest aspirations' for career development among working-class youth; constrained by what they think is possible and plausible in their context of understanding contemporary social risks. They continue to emphasise just having a job, a home and a family and being able to 'get by' as their core aspirations for work. Allen and Hollingworth (2013) explain this well in relation to the difficulty with which young people can conceive of a career in the creative industries, one of the areas held as the vanguard of the 'new' knowledge economy. By using a Bourdieusian position of recognising the socio-spatial dimensions of classed habitus, they suggest that '...class-based dispositional understandings [shape] what is thinkable for "people like me" but also for "people from round here" '. Similar issues are observed by Kintrea et al. (2015), who have shown that 'place' has a significant impact on people's social networks, identities and aspirations.

This relationship between class and employment possibilities was explicitly addressed in much early youth scholarship. Roberts (1968, 1995), for example, brought attention to local opportunity structure that has been followed by others. Research by Connolly and Healy (2004) also observes that working-class boys' locality played a central role in mediating their experiences and perspectives on their future work engagements. These social mechanisms are also captured by Hodkinson et al. (1996), who develop a Bourdieusian model of 'careership' and its related concept of 'horizons for action'. These were strongly influenced by a person's position, by the nature of the field or fields within which they are positioned and the embodied dispositions of the person him/herself (Hodkinson et al. 1996). This results in seemingly 'pragmatically rational' calculations by working-class youngsters, with a consequence being career orientations that may be at odds with the knowledge economy emphasis on both traditional and also emerging middle-class professions.

A most impressive account of how all of these issues combine is researched by MacDonald et al. (2005). Conducted in deprived (materially and educationally) areas of the North East of England, MacDonald et al. made clear the realities of the aforementioned formations of aspirations and its impact upon work over a period of time. First, they demonstrated the significance of the localisation of housing careers for employment careers. Neighbourhoods, combined with family and community, produced complex attachments to place, with local opportunity structures being key for employment. The employment that was then available in such areas was often routine low-skilled work in the lower reaches of the service sector or in factories (MacDonald et al. 2005). In many cases, supply of work outstripped demand in these areas, meaning that '...unemployment, job insecurity and poor work [were] common features of working class experiences of work' (881). The common thread of this experience of work is of crucial importance. Often political rhetoric has sought to imply that young people who are workless or who have little work have plenty of opportunity, but, as Roberts (2011) makes clear, this type of engagement with poor work is very typical among 'ordinary youth'. The notion of 'ordinary' is not used pejoratively to distance the most deprived sections of the working class, but to make the important point that among those who are not deemed most at risk, similar employment options prevail.

Who Gets 'Poor Work'?

The distribution of unemployment, underemployment and precarious work is not experienced the same by all young people. Those from the lowest SES groups or from families that have a history of poor work or long-term unemployment continue to encounter low-paid occupations and poor work (Simmons et al. 2014; France 2016). For example, research conducted by Shildrick et al. (2010) exploring the relationship young working-class people in Teesside, one of the most deprived areas in the UK, had with the local labour market showed:

> '...that overall [] levels of educational attainment did not predict improved labour market fortunes. Even the best qualified – those with degrees and diplomas – participated, at least at times, in 'low-pay, no-pay' churning labour market careers in the same ways as the least qualified (Shildrick et al. 2010: 5)

This research clearly illustrated that even when young people attained a degree (usually from their local university) or some other form of qualification – the recognised types of institutionalised cultural capital, as Bourdieu would have it – they were still destined for a life of 'low pay' and 'poor quality' work. Shildrick et al.'s interviewees experienced a 'churning' process between insecure, temporary work, unemployment and/or low-level training and skill development. Even those who went to university tended to return to find work locally but encountered a labour market with little to offer. This is an important reminder of how social capital must interlock with local occupational opportunities to be of value in these terms (who you know, and the possibilities they offer rather than how many you know, per se). Also, we see here that qualifications, of course, are not equally valued – processes of distinction are at work that position a degree from newer, vocationally oriented or more 'working-class universities' as inferior to degrees from elite or traditional (read, more middle class) institutions. Seemingly 'better' or 'lesser' reputations work to consolidate class advantage, becoming a source of capital in themselves – a capital embodied by institutions and internalised by individuals, and which sees the hierarchicalisation of knowledge become accepted.

As we identified in Chapter 3, although more young people now attend university, most working-class young people's post-school education is through pathways in the vocational sector (VET in the UK and New Zealand, and TAFE in Australia). Making the transition across into higher education is less likely once on the VET pathway, often making people 'trapped' into vocational skill development. A similar point is made by Tomlinson (2013) in her review of 'low attainers' in the global economy. She shows that in the USA, Germany, the UK, Malta and Finland being a 'low attainer' has a strong connection with being working class. Despite a recent diverse and complex restructuring of the field of post-16 training and education, the social reproduction of class trajectories has changed little. Upward social mobility, especially for those at the 'bottom of the pile' remains highly improbable. These features are not unique to the urban environment. Research in Australia (Cuervo and Wyn 2011) on young people's experience of work, education and training in rural areas showed that with the collapse of the rural labour market and the limited opportunities for quality, well-paid work, young people find themselves 'trapped' in local areas where transport to urban centres for work are limited and most work is temporary and insecure. In this context, those with the least resources are unable to avoid being churned through and around the system (Cuervo and Wyn 2011).

Differences Among Graduates

Clearly, working-class young people with few academic cultural and social resources and strong attachments to place in areas with weak opportunity structures might struggle in respect of employment relative to their middle-class counterparts. However, the ways in which graduates engage with and experience the labour market is also remarkably telling. Graduate qualifications provide an array of protections such as reduced chances of being unemployed, and higher salary returns over the working lifetime relative to lower educated peers. Correspondingly, however, graduate returns and experiences are highly unequal and the accurate point of comparison is *between* graduates. Research on differentials of outcomes of those who attend university has been sparse, although a growing body of evidence confirms significant differences exist among graduates in terms of who benefits most from going to university.

Those graduates from advantaged or privileged backgrounds (and particularly those who had been privately educated) achieve employment in higher status occupations and earn higher returns from their degree than their working-class peers (examples include Bukodi and Goldthorpe 2012; Crawford and Vignoles 2014; Britton et al. 2016). Being privately educated is significant and creates a premium over and above what could be expected by doing a degree. Crawford and Vignoles (2014), for example, showed that graduates who attended private secondary schools earned approximately 7% more per year, on average, than state school students 3.5 years after graduation, even when comparing otherwise similar graduates and controlling for differences in degree subject, university attended and degree classification. Relatedly, Britton et al.'s (2016) analysis of major administrative data showed that parental income remains a most significant feature in determining future career trajectories and incomes of young people after university. As a result, the average gap in earnings between students from higher- and lower-income backgrounds is £8,000 a year for men and £5,300 a year for women, 10 years after graduation (Britton et al. 2016). Status of the university attended also contributes to maintaining this inequality. As per Chapter 3, when young people from working-class backgrounds participate in higher education, they often cluster in particular university types, further increase the differential of outcomes and continue to reflect social class inequalities (this is significant for young people from different ethnic backgrounds; see Chapter 5). Variations in future incomes exist between those who attended elite and high-performing universities (i.e. the 'Russell Group') and the 'new' universities. Given most working-class young people attend the latter, earnings after leaving university are significantly lower. The bottom line is that social class background and the level of education attained by the parents of young graduates are very often very powerful predictors of labour market destinations (Britton et al. 2016; Jacob et al. 2015). While the complexity of such institutional inequality on returns is to do with university and course-based prestige and signalling mechanisms, it is augmented by other non-tangible benefits that students at elite universities accrue, and which also build upon their parents' economic, social and cultural capital.

Various studies show how these classed processes create different types of educational experience that enhance differentiated opportunities both within and after university. One example is the ability of those from wealthier backgrounds to develop their CV during and beyond university (Heath 2007). For example, the 'gap year' is seen as an important 'new form' of cultural capital that can and does bring added value to graduate CV. Traditionally, the 'gap year' was seen as 'time off' or a chance for personal growth, but the contemporary competitive environment has led to the professionalisation of travel, and a sense of instrumental purpose (Snee 2013). Rather than the 'gap year' being about 'unproductive' fun and leisure travel, neoliberal discourses place greater value on 'career development' possibilities and the production a 'public image' of self that is appealing to employers. Yet, 'gap years' remain dominated by the middle classes (Snee 2013; King 2011) who have both the economic resources and family support to facilitate this venture. As these types of activities gain greater institutional recognition, they prove to be a form of social distinction (King 2011). For example, Heath (2007) suggests gap years are a middle-class response to the widening participation agenda in higher education,[3] in that they help produce new forms of embodied cultural capital in the form of '...soft skills, greater maturity, enhanced self-awareness and increased independence' (Heath 2007: 100; see also; Snee 2013). This is advantageous when seeking graduate work.

Another good example comes from the work of Grugulis and Stoyanova's (2012) study of the film and TV industry. They explained how social capital advantaged white, middle-class men and ensured that middle-class signals came to be proxies for the most sought-after jobs. This kind of process often starts in universities, with middle-class students using their family-embedded social capital to access the best internships (Shade and Jacobson 2015; Bathmaker et al. 2013), and then within those same internships further strengthen their networks. Internships, indeed, have been identified across many nations as being critical for maintaining and developing advantage. Shade and Jacobson's (2015) study of Canadian graduates showed that internships in the 'creative sector' were dominated by those from more privileged backgrounds. Such opportunities tend to be 'employment-based', and lead to pay and more permanent work, yet there is a strong bias in who gets access to the best internships.

A recent report in the UK (Intergenerational Foundation 2014) showed that the most desirable and profitable internships were based in London, yet those from working-class backgrounds found it increasingly difficult not only to access them but also to live in London without any substantial income. As a result, most of the best internships went to young people who had families who financially support extended periods of unpaid intern experience. To secure a job, many young people need experience of more than one internship, but, again, working-class young people are less able to continue for longer periods of time without an income (Intergenerational Foundation 2014). These findings are re-enforced by Leonard et al.'s (2015) observations of complex rationalisations and mixed motivations for undertaking internships. They found that for young people internships were becoming the 'new degree' – the new must have form of differentiation for accessing good jobs – but that social class was again at work, with those from middle-class backgrounds feeling like 'a fish in water' and using substantial parental support to intern unpaid (Leonard et al. 2015).

The association between social class and employment outcomes has deeper roots than even university, with suggestions that contact with employers during school education leads to pupils being five times less likely to be NEET (Mann 2012). This same research shows that it is predominantly fee-paying private schools that have ongoing connections with industries to promote such network building and provide exposure. Statistical analyses of this phenomenon of social capital reveal a degree of complexity. Recent work from the UK by Macmillan and colleagues (2015) suggest there is a large, statistically significant socio-economic gradient in the likelihood of a recent graduate accessing a most prestigious occupation. However, they also found that socio-economically advantaged students are neither better qualified nor necessarily use their networks in order to access top jobs. They do note, however, that using professional networks to find a job, rather than some other method, enhances the likelihood of working in a top NS-SEC job by 5.3 percentage points. They further speculate that there is likely to have been some under reporting of using one's social network, due to suspicions by respondents that this might appear less meritorious. That said, a number of other studies have recently showed that class still matters in these processes. For example, Brown et al. (2010) showed that even though the number and diversity of university graduates have increased substantially, employers recruiting in the financial sector still recruit interns from the elite group of universities. The UK's Social Mobility Unit confirms this practice as relevant in terms of employment into the key professions, showing that graduate recruitment agencies tend to target the most elite universities that are also the most selective (e.g. Cambridge, Oxford, the London School of Economics, UCL and the University of Manchester) (Milburn 2012). Once again, class is critical to the process of graduate recruitment. This is more complex in the Australian case where wage data shows that recent graduates from non-elite institutions have the best wages and employment levels. Caution should be read here, however, as evidence still indicates that employers of higher level professions tend towards employing graduates from elite institutions, with close to 40% of Australian employers expressing a preference of university for their prospective employees (GCA 2016).

Allied to this is research on wage returns among upwardly mobile graduates in the UK (Friedman et al. 2015). Proposing the concept of a 'class ceiling', Friedman and colleagues demonstrated that significant wage inequality exists *within* elite occupational groups. Focussing on just the highest occupational social class, they show a clear gradient that implies a working-class background produces a wage penalty relative to those who were born into and remain in social class one when entering the labour market. They also found clear classed compositions of workforces, with the more traditionally middle-class professions tending to recruit predominantly graduates of middle-class origin, compared to technical industries, such as IT or engineering, which recruit more diversely. Replicate international research is very much needed.

Qualitative research has also repeatedly documented how class comes to impact negotiation and engagement with the graduate labour market in various ways. Matthys (2012), for instance, found conflicts between working-class origin and typically middle-class destinations. These conflicts lead to communication barriers and limitations on one's willingness to present as assertive, in many ways reflecting Bourdieu's 'fish out of water'. Social connections and cultural codes also have important impacts on obtaining certain types of jobs or roles, which in some ways speaks to the limits in wage capacity for the upwardly mobile identified by Friedman et al. (2015). Further complexity is unravelled by Abrahams's (2016) work on classed predispositions to nepotism. Abrahams argues that a commensurate fit between habitus and field sees middle-class graduates demonstrate absolute willingness to make the most of social networks to gain advantages in the labour market. Correspondingly, working-class students presented anxieties about such activity, positioning advantageous networks as morally unacceptable. Having imbibed the neoliberal discourses of individualism and meritocracy, instead they valued hard work and enterprise not only as means of standing out from the crowd but also as vital contributors to their sense of self-worth.

Such notions and their potential limitations have been explored through the lens of 'moral capital', showing how working-class graduates inscribe ideas of 'doing it by myself' and 'hard work' with a value that might not be recognised in the graduate labour market (Lehmann 2014; Roberts and Li 2016). These all points to how employability, 'with its emphasis on individual responsibility and neglect of social inequalities', has potentially damaging consequences for these working-class graduates (Moreau and Leathwood 2006). This is especially the case where employability is rendered a one-size-fits-all solution – employability should instead be recognised as comprising individual positions and dispositions, and the social contacts developed as part of undergraduate life and how these connect with (or not) specific workplace cultures and organisation.

Further constructions of advantage and privilege have been noted that are also intrinsically linked to class struggles. By adapting the sociological concept of social closure, Tholen (2016) proposes the idea of 'symbolic closure' as a way of understanding new forms of exclusion that operate in a context where simply having a university degree does not act as a necessary point of social distinction. That is, middle-class people turn their attention to differences within the graduate 'group'. In the field of employment, then, 'graduates are involved in occupations where the worth of the qualification and the graduate category needs to be (re)negotiated'. However, this process is an unequal undertaking because middle class '[d]omination resides in the power to allocate symbolic meaning to categories and labour and educational positions, identities and statuses' (2016: 13). For this reason, the overarching reality is that while more working-class young people have become graduates, they have not become more socially mobile. Instead, they remain concentrated in recently professionalised occupations, in part because of the practices of symbolic closure produced and practiced in combination by middle-class students and families, elite educational institutions and elite professions and occupations. The complicity in this process of inequality between institutions and organisations is well observed by Binder et al.'s (2016) study of US elite institutions, Harvard and Stanford, where students were funnelled into highly prestigious employment. Ultimately, those from less privileged backgrounds are not only less likely to enter elite universities, they may also have less cultural resources to legitimise their own educational and social trajectory, yet 'because the dominated internalize the social structure in which they exist, they do not recognize [this inequality] as such' (Burawoy 2012: 203).

The Importance of Family Economic Capital

Parents and others within the family network can and do offer access to a wide range of economic, social and cultural capital. As mentioned earlier, in terms of internships, both social capital and financial support from parents are critical for accessing the best opportunities. Within these processes there is also further significant transference of wealth and resource occurring across generations that is central to the maintenance of social class. This continues beyond education in that those from more privileged backgrounds have access to a wide range of capitals that can help mediate and smooth their movement into some form of independent adulthood. For example, research in New Zealand (Chapple et al. 2015) shows that by age 38, inequalities of wealth ownership between social groups are well established. Contrary to popular perception, those from wealthy backgrounds are accruing substantial wealth early in the life course ensuring that they will remain part of the future wealth-owning class. Druta and Ronald (2016) and Appleyard and Rowlingson (2010) also show how these processes are not just forms of intergenerational support but also about transferring wealth within family networks. This remains a critical way that families with substantial wealth ensure it stays within the family. What it also suggests is that rather than happening later in life or posthumously, much wealth transfer is now happening earlier (Chapple et al. 2015). However, such privilege and advantage is usually invisible and denied, existing within informal and formal practices that can be legitimised by intuitional and structural contexts. While there is some research in the UK and anecdotal evidence in New Zealand, there is little detailed research of how this process works and how it affects the disadvantaged and less privileged; yet, it is clear to us that class operates in this process. That young people's parents live longer does not necessarily impede access to family resources to the extent that some imply (e.g. Rayner 2016).

One of the most significant ways that parents and others help their children manage their transitions into adulthood is by 'gifting' financial resources. Researching a group of relatively privileged young people, Heath and Calvert (2013) found that 'gifting' was a very common practice amongst the middle class, sometimes being 'ad hoc' (giving the 'odd £20') or a special gift such as not only helping to buy bedding but also helping to 'bail' out of overdraft charges or covering expenses such as insurance and car tax payments. This 'gifting' can and does go beyond this to include paying regular monthly bills or rent. It also included, especially for the more wealthy, deposits for houses and associated costs (solicitor's fees). Grandparents also were making large financial 'gifts' to their grandchildren in the house-purchasing process (Heath and Calvert 2013). They go on to show that

> For those from more established middle-class families, the support that parents (and often grandparents) were able to provide often reinforced middle class advantage in a particularly powerful way, adding to the prospect of home ownership becoming ever more the preserve of the children of existing home owners (Health and Calvert, 2013: 1133)

Financial support also comes through parent's provision of accommodation for their children after they have left education. Many recent international studies have showed that large numbers of those young adults now live with their parents (Fry and Passel 2014; ABS 2013). For example, in Europe over 48% of those aged 18–30 now live at the parental home, during the GFC this trend increased in most European countries (Eurofound 2014). Countries such as Italy now see over 78% of all young people in this age group still living at home. A similar trend exists in Australia, where the proportion of young people aged 18–34 have never left home to live elsewhere increased by 4 percentage points to 31% since the start of the GFC.[4] Research suggests that inability to leave the parental home is closely related to class, but often in complicated ways. For instance, those more likely to be unemployed are more likely to be still living at home, and this is the same for almost all indicators of precarity (Berrington et al. 2014). As per our discussion on higher education in Chapter 3, these trends reflect that many working-class young people struggle to be mobile or take risks by going outside of their local geography. Home offers a cheap way of living and can help them manage some form of semi-independence, while not having enough resources to support independent living arrangements. Conversely, however, young people who are unemployed but come from families who are in receipt of benefits are more likely to leave home earlier than those from more privileged backgrounds (Cobb-Clark and Gørdens 2012). A better picture would be built by research that investigates the type of housing (public housing, private renting or purchased etc.) and also the locations of housing to better get a sense of the differences in this realm between classes. For example, Rugg (2010: 4) contends that young 'blue collar workers' might be left with 'less secure and less salubrious options' when it comes to house sharing, despite the growing incidence and almost normative expectation among young people, given that housing often becomes affordable for most young people only when costs are shared (Roberts 2013).

The process of leaving home is a far from linear one step process. Many young people are reliant on the family home, seeing it as a 'refuge' before 'relaunching' themselves. This strategy of what has been called the 'boomerang generation' has been increasing and involves young people moving in and out of the family home as a way of creating a safety net when things don't work out when trying to gain independence. For example, in a UK-based study (Sage et al. 2013), university graduates would move between five and eight times before they found permanent accommodation. Over one-third would initially return home and stay for over a year. From this base, many would move to other parts of the country in search of work but if unsuccessful would again return home. In fact, over 50% of young people returned to the family home in the first 5 years after leaving university. In this process, parents helped by making it a cheap option with over half of the young people not paying any rent or contributing to household bills or paying for meals. This is echoed in qualitative research in Australia conducted by Warner et al. (2016), which demonstrated that returning to the family home can be a rewarding and generally positive experience for graduates. Ultimately, though, families from higher SES groups are more able to offer levels and type of support that help smooth transitions to independent living, illustrated by the fact that they are more likely to leave home permanently sooner than those from lower SES groups (Stone et al. 2011; Druta and Ronald 2016). The pivotal point here is that class dis/advantage is compounded. While the likes of Rayner (2016) talk of the plight of Australia's 'generation less', in part because of rising house prices and the increasing disconnect form average wages, and even accepting that underemployment, precarity and so on affects more and more young people, the impact of this is heavily mediated by familial class-based resources.

Conclusion

We are continually surprised about the lack of systematic research into the classed nature of young people's encounters with the labour market. While interest in graduate employment and destinations, the growing precariousness of work, increased 'flexible' working and the growth of new 'gig' economy of self-employment have become more visible internationally, little discussion of these major social changes has been framed within a class analysis framework. This is ironic given the historical traditions of class theory (being focused on labour market relationships) and we have tried to show here Bourdieu's ideas can be fruitful invaluable for helping us make sense of the ways that social reproduction of class identities is taking place. Recognising the importance of fields gives youth sociologist's opportunities to explore in more detail the interplay between subfields and social practice, drawing together macro and micro process that are shaping locally based opportunities. Our analysis of the available research has shown that young people are in a highly competitive field with limited opportunities for success. In this context, individual and family capital (economic, social and cultural) come into their own. From the previous discussion it is those with a particular habitus and opportunities are able to better position themselves and accrue new forms of capitals (i.e. internships and CV's of international travel). They are in a stronger place to maintain a place in the top end of the class system. It is not 'luck' or 'chance' that helps the rich, the wealthy and the established middle class maintain their position; the class resources being made available between generations help their middle-class children navigate their way through the complex field of post-16 education, training and work.

Notes

1. See http://www.ilo.org/wcmsp5/groups/public/—dgreports/—dcomm/—publ/documents/publication/wcms_368626.pdf
2. See Hill (2013) for a discussion of why this was the case.
3. See Chapter 2 for related discussion of the New Zealand 'Overseas Experience' working holiday.
4. See http://www.abs.gov.au/ausstats/abs@.nsf

References

Abrahams, J. (2016). Honourable mobility or shameless entitlement? Habitus and graduate employment. *British Journal of Sociology of Education*, 1–13.

ABS (2013) *Australian Social Trends, April 2013*, http://www.abs.gov.au/AUSSTATS/abs@.nsf/Lookup/4102.0Main±Features40April±2013.

ABS (2016) *Characteristics of Employment, Australia, August 2015*, [numbers derived from Data Cube 14, available: http://www.abs.gov.au/AUSSTATS/abs@.nsf/DetailsPage/6333.0August%202015?OpenDocument]

Allen, K., & Hollingworth, S. (2013). 'Sticky subjects' or 'Cosmopolitan creatives'? Social class, place and urban young people's aspirations for work in the knowledge economy. *Urban Studies*, 50(3), 499–517.

Appleyard, L., & Rowlingson, K. (2010). *Home-ownership and the distribution of personal wealth*. York: Joseph Rowntree Foundation.

Ashton, D., & Field, D. (1976). *Young workers: From school to work*. London: Hutchinson.

Ashton, D. N., & Maguire, M. J. 1986. Young adults in the labour market. Department of Employment, Research Paper 55.

Atkinson, W. (2013). Class habitus and perception of the future: recession, employment insecurity and temporality. *The British Journal of Sociology*, 64(4), 643–661.

Autor, D. (2010). The polarization of job opportunities in the US labor market: Implications for employment and earnings. *Center for American Progress and The Hamilton Project*.

Bates, I., & Riseborough, G. (1993). *Youth and inequality*. Milton Keynes: Open University Press.

Bathmaker, A. M., Ingram, N., & Waller, R. (2013). Higher education, social class and the mobilisation of capitals: Recognising and playing the game. *British Journal of Sociology of Education*, 34(5–6), 723–743.

Berrington, A., Tammes, P., & Roberts, S. (2014) *Economic Precariousness and Living in the Parental Home in the UK*. CPC working paper, University of Southampton.

Binder, A. J., Davis, D. B., & Bloom, N. (2016). Career funneling: How elite students learn to define and desire "Prestigious" jobs. *Sociology of Education*, 89(1), 20–39.

Borlagdan, J. (2015). Inequality and 21-year-olds' negotiation of uncertain transitions to employment: A Bourdieusian approach. *Journal of Youth Studies*, 18(7), 839–854.

Brannen, J., & Nilsen, A. (2002). Young people's time perspectives: From youth to adulthood. *Sociology*, 36(3), 513–537.

Britton, J., Dearden, L., Shephard, N., & Vignoles, A. (2016). *How English domiciled graduate earnings vary with gender, institution attended, subject and socio-economic background* (No. W16/06). London: Institute for Fiscal Studies.

Brooks, R., & Everett, G. (2009). Post-graduation reflections on the value of a degree. *British Educational Research Journal, 35*(3), 333–349.

Brown, P., Lauder, H., & Ashton, D. (2010). *The global auction: The broken promises of education, jobs, and incomes.* Oxford: Oxford University Press.

Bukodi, E., & Goldthorpe, J. H. (2012). Decomposing 'social origins': The effects of parents' class, status, and education on the educational attainment of their children. *European Sociological Review, 29*(5), 1024–1039.

Burawoy, M. (2012). The Roots of domination: Beyond Bourdieu and Gramsci. *Sociology, 46*(2), 187–206.

Callender, C. (2008). The impact of term-time employment on higher education students' academic attainment and achievement. *Journal of Education Policy, 23*(4), 359–377.

Cannadine, D. (2000). *Class in Britain.* London: Penguin UK.

Carter, M. (1962). *Home, school and work.* Oxford: Pergamon.

Chapple, S., Hogan, S., Milne, B., Poulton, R., & Ramrakha, S. (2015). New Zealand's generation X. *Policy Quarterly, 11*(1), 73–78.

Chesters, J., O'Flaherty, M., & Western, J. (2007). Social Class and the Rise of the Self-Employed. In: Proceedings of TASA and SAANZ Joint Conference 2007. *TASA and SAANZ Joint Conference 2007,* Auckland New Zealand, (1–8). 4–7 December 2007.

Cobb – Clark, D., & Gorgens, T. (2012). *The capacity of families to support young Australians: financial transfers from parents, co-residence and youth outcomes,* Occasional Paper No. 45, (pp. 1-64). Canberra, Australia: Commonwealth of Australia.

Connolly, P., & Healy, J. (2004). Symbolic violence, locality and social class: The educational and career aspirations of 10-11 year old boys in Belfast. *Pedagogy, Culture and Society, 12*(1), 15–33.

Côté, J. E. (2014). Towards a new political economy of youth. *Journal of Youth Studies, 17*(4), 527–543.

Crawford, C., & Vignoles, A. (2014). *Heterogeneity in graduate earnings by socio-economic background.* London: Institute of Fiscal Studies.

Cuervo, H., & Wyn, J. (2011). Rethinking youth transitions in Australia: A historical and multidimensional approach. University of Melbourne: Melbourne.

Curtis, S., & Shani, N. (2002). The effect of taking paid employment during term-time on students' academic studies. *Journal of Further and Higher Education, 26*(2), 129–138.

Druta, O., & Ronald, R. (2016). Young adults' pathways into homeownership and the negotiation of intra-family support: A home, the ideal gift. *Sociology,* 0038038516629900.

Dwyer, P., Wilson, B., & Woock, R. R. (1984). *Confronting school and work: Youth and class cultures in Australia.* Australia: Allen and Unwin.

Eurofound. (2014). *Social situation of young people in Europe*. Luxembourg: Publications Office of the European Union.
France, A. (2016). *Understanding youth in the global economic crisis*. Bristol: Policy Press.
Friedman, G. (2014). Workers without employers: Shadow corporations and the rise of the gig economy. *Review of Keynesian Economics*, 2(2), 171–188.
Friedman, S., Laurison, D., & Miles, A. (2015). Breaking the 'class' ceiling? Social mobility into Britain's elite occupations. *The Sociological Review*, 63(2), 259–289.
Fry, R., & Passel, J. S. (2014). *In post-recession era, young adults drive continuing rise in multi-generational living*. Washington, DC: Pew Research Center.
Furlong, A., Woodman, D., & Wyn, J. (2011). Changing times, changing perspectives: Reconciling 'transition' and 'cultural' perspectives on youth and young adulthood. *Journal of Sociology*, 47(4), 355–370.
Furlong, A., Goodwin, J., Hadfield, S., Hall, S., Lowden, H., O'Connor, H., & Plugor, R. (2017). *Young people in the labour market: Past, present, future*. London: Routledge.
Gallie, D., & Paugam, S. (2002). Social Precarity and Social Integration: Report for the European Commission Based on Eurobarometer 56.1. Brussels: European Commission.
GCA (2016) *Graduate Outlook 2015*. Melbourne: Graduate Careers Australia. http://www.graduatecareers.com.au/wp-content/uploads/2016/07/Graduate-Outlook-Report-2015-FINAL1.pdf
Goodwin, J., & O'Connor, H. (2016). *Norbert Elias's lost research: Revisiting the young worker project*. Farnham: Ashgate.
Goos, M., Manning, A., and Salomons, A. (2010). Explaining job polarisation in Europe: the roles of technology, globalisation and institutions. *London: LSE (CEP Discussion paper, No 1026)*.
Grugulis, I., & Stoyanova, D. (2012). Social capital and networks in film and TV: Jobs for the boys? *Organization Studies*, 33(10), 1311–1331.
Heath, S. (2007). Widening the gap: Pre-university gap years and the 'economy of experience'. *British Journal of Sociology of Education*, 28(1), 89–103.
Heath, S., & Calvert, E. (2013). Gifts, loans and intergenerational support for young adults. *Sociology*, 47(6), 1120–1135.
Hill, J. (2013) Why did Australia fare so well in the Global Financial Crisis?, *The CLS Blue Sky Blog*, February 7th, 2013. http://clsbluesky.law.columbia.edu/2013/02/07/why-did-australia-fare-so-well-in-the-global-financial-crisis/
Hodkinson, P., Sparkes, A., & Hodkinson, H. (1996). Triumphs and tears. *Young People, Markets and the Transition from School to Work, Manchester Metropolitan University Education Series, David Fulton, London*.

Humpage, L. (2016). Income management in New Zealand and Australia: Differently framed but similarly problematic for Indigenous peoples. *Critical Social Policy*, 0261018316638459.

Intergenerational Foundation. (2014). *Young people and employment*. London: Intergenerational Foundation.

Jacob, M., Klein, M., & Iannelli, C. (2015). The impact of social origin on graduates' early occupational destinations—An Anglo-German comparison. *European Sociological Review*, *31*(4), 460–476.

Jaimovich, N., & Siu, H. E. (2012). *The trend is the cycle: Job polarization and jobless recoveries* (No. w18334). National Bureau of Economic Research.

Jewell, S. (2014). The impact of working while studying on educational and labour market outcomes. *Business and Economics Journal*, *5*(3), 1–12.

Jones, K., Brinkley, I., & Crowley, L. (2015). *Going Solo: Does self-employment offer a solution to youth unemployment?* Lancaster: The Work Foundation.

Kalleberg, A. L. (2009). Precarious work, insecure workers: Employment relations in transition. *American Sociological Review*, *74*(1), 1–22.

King, A. (2011). Minding the gap? Young people's accounts of taking a gap year as a form of identity work in higher education. *Journal of Youth Studies*, *14*(3), 341–357.

Kintrea, K., St Clair, R., & Houston, M. (2015). Shaped by place? Young people's aspirations in disadvantaged neighbourhoods. *Journal of Youth Studies*, *18*(5), 666–684.

Laughland-Booÿ, J., Mayall, M., & Skrbiš, Z. (2015). Whose choice? Young people, career choices and reflexivity re-examined. *Current Sociology*, *63*(4), 586–603.

Lehmann, W. (2014). Habitus transformation and hidden injuries: Successful working-class university students. *Sociology of Education*, *87*(1), 1–15.

Leonard, P., Halford, S., & Bruce, K. (2015). 'The New Degree?' Constructing internships in the third sector. *Sociology*, 0038038515574456.

Levitas, R. (2005). The inclusive society? Social exclusion and new labour. Second edition. Basingstoke: Palgrave Macmillan.

MacDonald, R. (ed.) (1999). *Youth, the underclass and social exclusion*. London: Routledge.

MacDonald, R., & Coffield, F. (1990). *Risky business?: Youth and the enterprise culture*. Routledge.

MacDonald, R., & Marsh, J. (2005). *Disconnected youth?* Basingstoke: Palgrave.

MacDonald, R., Mason, P., Shildrick, T., Webster, C., Johnston, L., & Ridley, L. (2001). Snakes and ladders: In defence of studies of youth transition. *Sociological Research Online*, *5*(4). http://socresonline.org.uk/5/4/macdonald.html.

MacDonald, R., Shildrick, T., & Furlong, A. (2014). In search of 'intergenerational cultures of worklessness': Hunting the Yeti and shooting zombies. *Critical Social Policy*, 34(2), 199–220.

MacDonald, R., Shildrick, T., Webster, C., & Simpson, D. (2005). Growing up in poor neighbourhoods the significance of class and place in the extended transitions of 'socially excluded' young adults. *Sociology*, 39(5), 873–891.

Macmillan, L., Tyler, C., & Vignoles, A. (2015). Who gets the top jobs? The role of family background and networks in recent graduates' access to high-status professions. *Journal of Social Policy*, 44(3), 487–515.

Maguire, M., & Maguire, S. (1999). Young people and the labour market. In R. MacDonald (ed.), *Youth, the underclass and social exclusion* (pp. 26–38). London: Routledge.

Mann, A. (2012). *It's who you meet: Why employer contacts at school make a difference to the employment prospects of young adults*. London: Education and Employers Taskforce.

Martin, E., & McCabe, S. (2007). Part-time work and postgraduate students: Developing the skills for employment? *Journal of Hospitality, Leisure, Sport and Tourism Education*, 6(2), 29–40.

Mathieson, J., Popay, J., Enoch, E., Escorel, S., Hernandez, M., Johnston, H., & Rispel, L. (2008) *Social Exclusion: Meaning, measurement and experience and links to health inequalities – A review of literature*. WHO Social Exclusion Knowledge Network Background Paper 1, WHO Publishing.

Matthys, M. (2012). *Cultural capital, identity, and social mobility: The life course of working-class university graduates*. London: Routledge.

McDonald, P., Pini, B., Bailey, J., & Price, R. (2011). Young people's aspirations for education, work, family and leisure. *Work, Employment and Society*, 25(1), 68–84.

McDowell, L. (2012). Post-crisis, post-Ford and post-gender? Youth identities in an era of austerity. *Journal of Youth Studies*, 15(5), 573–590.

Milburn, A. (2012). *University challenge: How higher education can advance social mobility*. London: HMSO.

Miles, S. (2000). *Youth lifestyles in a changing world*. New York: McGraw-Hill.

Moreau, M. P., & Leathwood, C. (2006). Graduates' employment and the discourse of employability: A critical analysis. *Journal of Education and Work*, 19(4), 305–324.

Muntaner, C., Borrell, C., Vanroelen, C., Chung, H., Benach, J., Kim, I. H., & Ng, E. (2010). Employment relations, social class and health: A review and analysis of conceptual and measurement alternatives. *Social Science and Medicine*, 71(12), 2130–2140.

Murray, C. (1990). *The emerging British underclass*. London: Institute of Economic Affairs.

Patton, W., & Smith, E. (2009). Part-time work of high school students and impact on educational outcomes. *Australian Journal of Guidance and Counselling*, *19*(02), 216–224.

Pollock, G. (2008). Youth transitions: Debates over the social context of becoming an adult. *Sociology Compass*, *2*(2), 467–484.

Rayner, J. (2016). *Generation less: How Australia is cheating the young*. Carlton: Black Inc.

Richardson, J. J., Kemp, S., Malinen, S., & Haultain, S. A. (2013). The academic achievement of students in a New Zealand university: Does it pay to work? *Journal of Further and Higher Education*, *37*(6), 864–882.

Roberts, K. (1968). The entry into employment: An approach towards a general theory. *The Sociological Review*, *16*(2), 165–182.

Roberts, K. (1995). *Youth and employment in modern Britain*. Oxford: OUP.

Roberts, S. (2011). Beyond 'NEET' and 'tidy' pathways: Considering the 'missing middle' of youth transition studies. *Journal of Youth Studies*, *14*(1), 21–39.

Roberts, S. (2013). Youth studies, housing transitions and the 'missing middle': Time for a rethink?. *Sociological Research Online*, *18*(3), 11.

Roberts, S., & Evans, S. (2013). 'Aspirations' and imagined futures: The im/possibilities for Britain's young working class. In W. Atkinson, S. Roberts & M. Savage (eds.), *Class inequality in austerity Britain* (pp. 70–89). Basingstoke: Palgrave Macmillan.

Roberts, S., & Li, Z. (2016). Capital limits: Social class, motivations for term-time job searching and the consequences of joblessness among UK university students. *Journal of Youth Studies*, 1–18.

Rokicka, M. (2014). *The impact of students' part-time work on educational outcomes* (No. 2014-42). Institute for Social and Economic Research.

Rugg, J. (2010). *Young people and housing: The need for a new policy agenda*. York: Joseph Rowntree Foundation.

Sage, J., Evandrou, M., & Falkingham, J. (2013). Onwards or homewards? Complex graduate migration pathways, well-being and the "parental safety net". *Population, Space and Place*, 19(6), 738–755.

Satterlee, L. (2009) *A case study of undergraduate student employment at a private university: Exploring the effects of social class and institutional context*, PhD Thesis, University of Maryland, available at http://pqdtopen.proquest.com/doc/304925003.html?FMT=ABS

Shade, L. R., & Jacobson, J. (2015). Hungry for the job: Gender, unpaid internships, and the creative industries. *The Sociological Review*, *63*(S1), 188–205.

Shildrick, T., MacDonald, R., Webster, C., & Garthwaite, K. (2010). *The low-pay, no-pay cycle*. York: Joseph Rowntree Foundation.

Simmons, R., Thompson, R., & Russell, L. (2014). *Education, work and social change: Young people and marginalization in post-industrial Britain*. Springer.

Skeggs, B. (2004). *Class, self, culture*. London: Routledge.
Snee, H. (2013). Framing the Other: Cosmopolitanism and the representation of difference in overseas gap year narratives. *The British Journal of Sociology, 64*(1), 142–162.
Standing, G. (2011). *The precariat: The new dangerous class*. London: A and C Black.
Stone, J., Berrington, A., & Falkingham, J. (2011). The changing determinants of UK young adults' living arrangements. *Demographic Research, 25*, 629–666.
Sukarieh, M., & Tannock, S. (2015). *Youth rising? The politics of youth in the global economy*. London: Routledge.
Sukarieh, M., & Tannock, S. (2016). On the political economy of youth: A comment. *Journal of Youth Studies, 19*(9), 1281–1289.
Tholen, G. (2016). Symbolic closure: Towards a renewed sociological perspective on the relationship between higher education, credentials and the graduate labour market. *Sociology*, online ahead of print.
Tomlinson, S. (2013). *Ignorant yobs? Low attainers in a global knowledge economy*. London: Routledge.
Vickers, M., Lamb, S., & Hinkley, J. (2003). *Student workers in high school and beyond: The effects of part-time employment on participation in education, training and work*. Camberwell: ACER.
Vickerstaff, S. (2003). Apprenticeship in the golden age': Were youth transitions really smooth and unproblematic back then?. *Work, Employment and Society, 17*(2), 269–287.
Wacquant, L. (2007). Pierre Bourdieu. In R. Stones (Ed.), *Key sociological thinkers* (pp. 261–277). (2nd ed.), London: Macmillan.
Warner, E., Henderson-Wilson, C., & Andrews, F. (2016). 'You just accept': Australian parents' and young adults' feelings towards returning to co-residence. *Families, Relationships and Societies*.
Willis, P. E. (1977). *Learning to labour: How working class kids get working class jobs*. New York: Columbia University Press.
Woodman, D. (2012). Life out of synch: How new patterns of further education and the rise of precarious employment are reshaping young people's relationships. *Sociology, 46*(6), 1074–1090.
Woodman, D., & Wyn, J. (2015). *Youth and generation: Rethinking change and inequality in the lives of young people*. London: Sage.
Wyn, J., & Woodman, D. (2006). Generation, youth and social change in Australia. *Journal of Youth Studies, 9*(5), 495–514.

CHAPTER 5

Youth, Class and Intersectionality

Abstract A major criticism of class studies has been that in prioritising class other inequalities are marginalised and given less attention. This logic has (perhaps inadvertently) been influential in marginalising class in the analysis of young people's lives. We suggest that recent theoretical and empirical developments in sociology that use a Bourdieusian approach can show the intersection between class and other inequalities, and illuminate how class changes the very nature and experiences of other inequalities. We suggest that by drawing on these approaches youth sociology could also gain greater insight into the intersection of class for indigenous populations such as the young New Zealand Māori and young people from Australian Aboriginal and Torres Strait backgrounds.

Keywords Youth · Intersectionality · Class · Gender · Race · Indigenous · Māori · Aboriginal and Torres Strait

YOUTH, SOCIAL CHANGE AND INEQUALITIES *BEYOND* CLASS

So far we have paid attention to the ways social class shapes young people's lives in a very pervasive and influential manner. Our approach in this chapter is not only to outline other inequalities that characterise young people's lives but also to draw attention to the lack of significance for youth studies of the notion of intersectionality – a way of trying to understand the interrelationship between inequalities that was brought into

© The Author(s) 2017
A. France, S. Roberts, *Youth and Social Class*,
DOI 10.1057/978-1-137-57829-7_5

sociology in the 1990s. We argue that more holistic intersectional analyses could and should serve youth sociology well. Before we get to that, however, we first address developments that have brought attention to other forms of difference beyond social class, and explore youth sociology's oversight of class in discussions of both gender and race.

One of the major changes over the last 30 years has been young women's significantly increased participation in education, training and paid work. That said, there remain significant divisions that show class is still at play. Prior to the 1990s, young men dominated participation in university, but by the 1990s across the advanced economies and especially in countries such as the UK, Australia and New Zealand, their participation was equal to young women's. With women's participation growing steadily, now over 25 countries (out of 30 industrialised nations) have higher education systems that contain more young women than men. Countries such as Ireland (65%), Norway (60%) and New Zealand (60%) have seen the biggest 'gaps' emerge (Lancrin 2008). That said, little has changed over the subjects studied, where gender segregation persists. Young women still tend to do education, the arts, humanities and health while young men do science, engineering and medicine (Barone 2011). But class is also still in play; young women entering the most prestigious areas (such as Law and medicine) tend to be from the middle classes. Enrolment figures continually show very low numbers of young women from low SES groups enter these areas of study (Equality Challenge Unit 2013). Similar patterns remain in vocational training. While opportunities are growing for young women to access apprenticeships, they still tend to do traditional 'female' activities such as hairdressing, social care and health, whereas young men do ICT and construction (France 2016). Similar to what we saw in Chapter 3, the young women who enter the VET sector tend to be from low SES groups. Evidence also shows that when these young women enter VET they are also paid less than young men, especially in areas such as apprenticeships (Fong and Phelps 2007). What we see, therefore, is a 'double whammy' for young women – disadvantage is compounded because of both their gender and also their class position.

In respect of paid employment, gender and class also remain significant. For example, the restructuring of youth transitions and the growing feminisation of the labour market is creating major challenges for young people (McDowell 2012). As we saw in Chapter 4, the modes of economy that facilitated traditional social reproduction that was evident in the work of Willis (1977) have virtually evaporated, but new forms have emerged. As large-scale manufacturing has disappeared the real area of growth in jobs has been in the service sector and in jobs traditionally done by young women (France 2016). As a result, more young women are entering work, although they are also more vulnerable to part-time, casual and precarious work than young men across the UK, Australia and New Zealand (France 2016). Again, being a young woman from a low SES grouping is likely to have a significant impact on incomes and opportunities. One of the other effects has been that young men, especially working-class young men, are now faced with less work opportunities in traditional areas such as manufacturing with more opportunities in areas seen traditionally as 'women's work'. Working in hospitality, in caring professions and retail along with having to do more part-time work and shift work is, as we shall see, challenging especially to young working-class men (McDowell 2012).

When considering the 'race' question it is important, for our purposes, to recognise differences between the UK and Australia and New Zealand. First, the relationship that the UK has with race is very much shaped by being a colonising nation which, for example, saw large numbers of migrants arrive from places such as the West Indies and India in the 1970s. Australia and New Zealand's major race question relates to how indigenous populations experienced colonialism in their home lands. This is not to deny that migration and the movement of the young across borders also remains important, but that these issues around indigeneity are fundamental to the history of both countries. These differences have historically been significant to how race and their relationship to the class question has been experienced in this different context.

In the UK, one of the most important trends on this issue is that the participation levels of almost all minority ethnic groups in higher education has risen substantially. For example, Black African young people are almost 35% more likely to go to university than otherwise-identical White British pupils, while most other ethnic minority groups are around 15–25% more likely to go than similar White British pupils (Crawford and Greaves 2015). Issues such as English as a first language and proximity to London increase the chances of minority students going to university compared to White British young people. Interestingly, a minority ethnic young person's SES is not such a predictor of university entry. In fact, all ethnic minorities in the lowest SES quintile group are, on average, significantly more likely to go to university than White British pupils in the same SES group (Crawford and Greaves 2015). This raises some pertinent questions regarding the relationship between class and race, which we explore in the following.

In terms of employment for ethnic minority graduates, race and class clearly have an impact. Ethnic minority graduates, for example, are more likely to be overqualified for their jobs than white graduates (Brynin and Longhi 2015), and across England and Wales ethnic minority groups are systematically under-represented in intermediate occupations (Catney and Sabater 2015). Young people from Black Caribbean backgrounds also have the lowest rate of professional employment six months after graduation. Forty months after leaving higher education the difference between the highest and lowest professional employment rates have widened to 13.2 percentage points. Black African qualifiers had the lowest rate at this stage of graduates' early careers, while Asian Indian and White qualifiers have the highest rates (HEFCE 2015). But the problem is not simply graduate employment. Historically, ethnicity has a close correlation with class in that large numbers of minority ethnic people have low incomes (Hudson et al. 2013) and suffer an ethnic pay penalty (Heath and Cheung 2007), with Bangladeshis, Pakistanis and migrant workers being over-represented in the minimum wage UK workforce (Low Pay Commission 2014). Recent research has showed that most British minority groups have been disproportionally affected by the growth of precarious work especially since the recession (TUC 2014). For example, temporary work, part-time work and the involvement in agency work and low-paid occupations grew faster amongst black and minority ethnic (BME) groups than any other group (TUC 2014). Not only are these groups affected disproportionally, but also it is young people who are hit the hardest. Throughout the recession, young BME people aged 18–24 who were 'unemployed for a year or more' increased by 49%, with rates of casualisation at almost double that of young white workers. Meanwhile, those unemployed aged 20–29 are also almost twice as likely to be from BME groups (TUC 2014).

When it comes to young Māori in New Zealand and Aboriginal and Torres Strait young people in Australia, it is important to recognise that colonialism has massively damaged their lives and life chances. Historically, colonialism set about destroying then assimilating these indigenous groups into a white colonial world. In this process their culture and language has been threatened with extinction and opportunities to improve themselves have been restricted. As a result, the starting point for many young people is at the bottom of the SES scales (France 2016). Over the last 20 plus years, New Zealand and Australian governments have announced programmes across education and work that claim to address their social disadvantage, yet little has changed. Young Māori and Aboriginal and Torres Strait people tend to be hit hardest by unemployment, to be employed in the lowest paid work and be working in the least secure jobs. Even though the GFC had a less detrimental effect in the antipodes than in the UK, youth unemployment and underemployment has still been rising fairly steadily, with indigenous populations hit much harder. Indigenous groups also have the lowest numbers and proportions entering university, yet also highest proportions of attrition and they are more likely to go into vocational training and/or end with the lowest levels of education (France 2016). For example, in a review of key indicators of social change (such as income, employment participation in tertiary education) in New Zealand between 2003 and 2013 it was showed:

> worsening outcomes for Māori and Pacific people in the form of increasing gaps in indicators when compared to the European population. Moreover, some of the indicators that produce improving outcomes still retain large gaps between the European population and Māori or Pacific people (Marriot and Sim 2015: 45)

Class, Gender and Youth Sociology

In understanding how the relationship between class and gender has been theorised within youth sociology, it is important to locate it in a historical context. The first issue we need to recognise is that youth sociology, as outlined in Chapter 2, emerged out of concerns not only about class but also about the behaviour and actions of white working-class boys (France 2007). In early studies of youth, girls were 'silent' and almost totally absent from a large part of youth sociology. For example, the Chicago School set itself out to explore why working-class boys committed more crime than middle-class boys (see also Burt 1925). Girls were not completely invisible, but when they were included the focus of interest was on the differences in nature between boys and girls and, particularly, around biology and sexuality, with both being seen as 'causal factors' of their respective behaviour (Smart 1976). Women's biology was seen to 'naturally' position them as chaste and pure, with deviations from this viewed as 'unnatural' and in some way intimately linked to sexual misconduct. These two assumptions about gender were dominant in a wide range of early studies of girls (France 2007).

Questions of class and gender became more central to debates in youth sociology in the 1970s, largely emerging from critiques of the Centre for Contemporary Cultural Studies (CCCS) work on youth subcultures, which had been fundamentally concerned with questions of class. Angela McRobbie (1978) suggested that CCCS scholars had given little attention to gender, arguing that much of the subcultural analysis of the 1970s and especially of the work of Willis (1977) was characterised by male researchers doing research on young men. Women and girls, for McRobbie, were discussed merely as appendages, with gender lacking the emphasis it deserved as a structural constraint that – similar to class – affected life chances. For McRobbie, Willis should have conducted a broader analysis of patriarchal family structures, and argued that Willis failed to recognise that the lads' behaviour and language was extremely sexist and re-enforced patriachical divisions. McRobbie went on to undertake a 'Willis' equivalent study of working-class girls, showing how growing up as a girl in a working-class neighbourhood was significantly differed to growing up as a boy (1978). In addition, though, by moving the analytical focus to girls' friendship groups, McRobbie made clear how these were a site for mutual support and the generation of capacities that allow working-class girls to cope with patriarchal subordination. Similar work was done by Christine Griffin (1985) in her UK-based study *Typical Girls*, which focused on the transition to work. Griffin showed how working-class girls had to manage the competing pressures of transitioning into both the labour market and marriage market, often resulting in low-paid and low-status work.

As we noted at the book's outset, concerns about the collapse of the youth labour market and the growth of the training state in the 1990s brought about new research on the forms of social reproduction for young people (e.g. Finn 1987; Hollands 1990). A number of these studies explored explicitly the impact these changes were having on working-class young women. For example, Bates researched girls who were training to be 'care girls' (Bates 1993a) and 'fashion designers' (1993b) in the new vocational training courses in the UK. She showed how young women's aspirations were both 'cooled' and reconfigured to fit into traditional female industries, reconfirming the gendered career pathways of old in 'new' times. Similarly, Roberts et al. (1994), examining young working-class women's youth transitions in Germany and the UK, showed that despite being more self-consciousness about themselves and their career directions, this did not lead them to challenge traditional gender stereotypes. Such research drew attention to the relationship between class and gender, but much of it *assumed* class as a feature of young people's lives rather than theorising class as a category or showing how it operated across different classed groups (i.e. the middle or upper class). The focus remained on those most disadvantaged located at the bottom of the economic pile.

Two major shifts in direction emerged in the study of gender in the early 2000s. Firstly, the 'cultural turn' and the growing influence of post-structuralism shifted the focus away from the activities of working-class young women to concentrate on exploring identity politics. In this, class seemed to have less relevance when considering the lives of young women. Secondly, it is at this point that Connell's (2005) work in the field of masculinity studies started to have an increasing impact on the sociology of youth and where studies of class and gender re-emerged. As per Chapter 2, the 'cultural turn' had a significant impact on (youth) sociology, shifting emphasis from the role of structural and institutional arrangements to the examination of cultural practice. This was evident in the book *Club Cultures* by Sarah Thornton (1995), which introduced a Bourdieusian concept of 'taste cultures', suggesting that club-goers congregate around shared music tastes and their common media interests rather than class interests. This in many ways marked the beginning of a body of work concentrating on consumption rather than production, arguing for a focus on exploring 'agency' and 'identity work' for young women. For example, Nava and Nava (1992) prioritised questions of how consuming practices construct feminine identities. Research that followed highlighted how girls engaged with concepts such as 'girl power' and how these positioned girls as '... feisty, ambitious, motivated and independent' (Aapola et al. 2005: 26), challenging notions of girls as passive. Within these studies class is acknowledged as important; yet, the main focus shifted to gender identity and cultural practice and in effect, sometimes inadvertently, aided the marginalisation of class analysis in youth sociology.

A massive expansion of work followed that explored femininity and/or 'girlhood', arguing what it means to be a girl in this post-structural age was being culturally re-defined. Studies explicitly examining young women's relationship to class or even to structure diminished and we learned increasingly less about young women's relationship with the labour market, their economic position in society or even the class-based resources that come to structure existence, largely in favour of Judith Butler–inspired analysis of post-modern identities. The most significant deviation from what was an emerging trend came from Walkerdine et al. (2001), in their study *'Growing Up Girl'*. Using a Bourdieusian framework, they showed how class and gender operated in schools, providing a vivid account of how femininity is regulated in very different ways for working-class girls compared to their middle-class peers. Others, while not addressing class processes, per se, took to task the idea that girls are paragons of neoliberal success. Anita Harris (2004), for instance, provided an example of this by comparing young women's apparent successes with the many young women who had limited educational qualifications, poor housing, no jobs or low-paid temporary work.

The second major development was the growing influence of masculinity studies (France 2007). While it was developed as a more nuanced reading of what it meant to be a boy in late modernity, class was, unlike in studies of girls, still a relevant question within debates – especially in education. This work was progressively interested in masculinity being 'in crisis' (Roberts 2014), 'uncertain' (O'Donnell and Sharpe 2002) and/or 'redundant' (McDowell 2003). Much of this work was on schooling, but identity formation and discourse analysis of the 'underachievement of boys' in education, alongside the examinations of the cultural practice of boys in the school setting were all seen as having relationships to class. Indeed, it is working-class boys' (dis)engagement from and aspirations for education, in particular, that is a perennial concern for policy makers and academics. Other education-based research has been influential. Archer and Yamashita's (2003) work was pivotal in exposing the range of masculine identities available from a cultural entanglement of various social factors such as ethnicity, sexuality and locality. Relatedly, studies have also explored differences within and between classes. For example, Ingram (2009) explored the tensions experienced in traversing school and community for working-class boys at Grammar schools in Northern Ireland, while Francis (1999) highlighted how 'laddish behaviour' was appropriated by middle-class boys in the school setting.

Research also paid attention to masculinity beyond education, with the stand-out example being McDowell's (2003) concentration on the impact restructuring of the labour market has upon young working-class masculinities. McDowell suggests that the shift to the service economy was reconstituting what it means to be a man. The types of jobs being developed demanded particular attributes that are problematic for young working-class males and as a result masculinity was changing for them (see also Nixon 2009). Becoming a man, therefore, involved a complex negotiation of traditional, localised forms of 'hegemonic masculinity', and changes in employment opportunities (McDowell 2003). Studies of masculinity and class have also concentrated on geography (e.g. Nayak 2003 on Newcastle; Ward 2015 on South Wales), highlighting the tensions brought about by social change that inform not only how working-class boys manage their masculinity, but also how multiple social characteristics intersect to inform this process. Excavations of the relationship between ethnicity and masculinity are evident, for example, on work about Muslim boys by the likes of Hopkins (2006) and Archer (2003); with the latter notably contending that despite it being hard to address multiple sources of identity and inequality, academics have a responsibility to always try (Archer 2003: 168). Furthermore, Roberts (2013) has also paid attention to complications in masculinity theorising, noting how 'ordinary' working-class young men, unlike those in McDowell's research, can negotiate masculinity in 'new times' with relative ease and operate without being disparaging or dismissive of seemingly feminised jobs. So while masculinity studies has developed a strong focus on youth identities, there has remained a continual interest in class (often more explicitly than in girls' studies). This, as we show later in the chapter, has been further enhanced by research drawing upon the work of Bourdieu.

Race and Class in Youth Sociology

The history of youth, class and race in sociology has its roots in early criminological work on the 'problem' of young migrants living in traditional white working-class communities. Despite some more critical and radical work that challenged this framework, this starting place remains a major feature and has influenced a wide range of studies that explored racialised process and practices. Much of this early work drew on advocates of eugenics, where real and observable differences were argued to be detected between the 'races'; these were held as the basis of the development of different cultures (Griffin 1993). Therefore, according to this formulation, just as *Homo sapiens* triumphed in the survival of the fittest, the emergence of Western Europe and North America as global forces was testament to perceived racial superiority of white Anglo-Saxons. Such arguments, while not always explicit, remain a feature of how different racial minority groups are perceived in both public and political discourses (Gilroy 1987).

More critical sociological accounts obviously approach these issues with considerable scrutiny, by setting out to challenge such perspectives and fully explore the relationship between race and class. For example, in criminology, writing in the tradition of the New Left, Lea and Young (1984) positioned growth in crime rates amongst black youth as a consequence of economic marginalisation: being poor, unemployed and living in poor housing were seen as pivotal. While such a perspective raised concerns, it highlighted that some form of relationship exists between economic disadvantage and race. Others, such as Gilroy (1987), argued the criminalisation of black youth in the UK reflected the deep-seated racism which infiltrates every corner of the criminal justice system. Similar arguments emerged in response to the public disorders in the UK during the 1980s. The (liberal) Scarman Report (1981) denied that a 'race riot' had taken place in Brixton, but did make the connection between the anger and resentment of young black people, in the context of a multitude of deprivations, and their relationship to the police. The report concluded that the Brixton riots was an outcome of a range of inter-connected factors associated with social inequality, racial discrimination and policing, which, added together, created a predisposition towards violence on the part of the black youth involved. Yet, clearly these young people involved in the 'riots' were economically marginalised and living alongside white working-class youth. It would, therefore, seem that the disturbances could only be understood by a model that recognised both race and class inequality.

Attempts to pathologise black culture and the characteristics of individual black people and their communities (i.e. labelling them the 'ghettos') represented important features of 'dealing' with the disorders. Images of black young people as the bearers of cultural values and attitudes, which not only reflected the depression and chaos of inner city areas, but also contained 'alien', imported values, remained the backdrop against which much debate occurred. The history of how these inner city areas became socially and economically blighted was largely ignored and the idea of violence and collective protest as an aberration, generated by the peculiarities of inner city life, was maintained and reproduced.

Another major development in youth sociology, again related to the emergence of post-structuralism, was the growing influence of 'difference' especially in relation to race. Probably the best starting place for this discussion is the work of Dick Hebdige (1979). Unlike many contemporaries, Hebdige was preoccupied with race rather than class. He suggested that British youth culture had within it embedded racist reactions to black youth. So, skinhead culture, for instance, could not be fully understood without considering issues of race. Hebdige (1979) suggested that Rastafarism became a 'style' constructed as a form of resistance to British imperialism and that having dreadlocks, smoking ganga, wearing khaki camouflage and listening to reggae became symbols of resistance. Griffin (2011) argues that the 1980s saw less focus on acts of 'resistance' as important underpinnings of youth cultural activities and a stronger focus on 'collusion' in debates over the relationship between structure, culture and agency, with the emphasis within post-structuralism, obviously, being culture and agency. Writers like Gilroy (1987) suggested that what might be fundamentally different was that the structural component of social relationships should be understood not just in terms of class but also in terms of colonialist history, institutionalised responses to race and global forces. It was claimed that the focus on local or national identities and cultural practices was becoming inappropriate. What then emerged was a stronger focus within cultural studies on how black youth construct themselves, achieved through an analysis of content, form, expression and dissent. Black youth were (and are), therefore, critical producers (as well as consumers) of culture (Meer and Nayak 2015). Within these discussions race is equated and given equal importance to material position and class is seen as less important.

The situation in both Australia and New Zealand is more complicated, but also shares some notable resonances with the UK. Where young black British populations, and their associated (and sometimes presumed) 'imported' cultural differences, are in part demonised or 'othered' through reference to the legacy of being second or third generation immigrants, indigenous populations similarly othered and considered culturally inferior as a result of the colonisation process. As we note in Chapter 2, the history of this process has left indigenous communities economically and culturally disenfranchised in ways that disproportionately situate them at the bottom rungs of the class hierarchy. As a disenfranchised group, indigenous youth in Australia and New Zealand, like black youth in the UK, are drastically over-represented in the criminal justice system.[1] For example, Māori comprise 14.6% of New Zealand's population but a staggering 51% of its prison population. Within this racialised reality there also exists disproportionate levels of incarceration for Māori and Pacific Islander descendants who live in Australia (Shepherd and Ilalio 2016). While some work addresses ways to best stem the 'pipeline' from school to the criminal justice system (Gordon 2015), and even identifies issues of job insecurity and other forms of economic disadvantage for indigenous youth (Shepherd and Ilalio 2016), marginalisation in relation to class appears to be much less of a priority than issues of belonging and cultural alienation. Such issues are related, and we take up this issue in more detail towards the end of the chapter.

INTERSECTIONALITY: FINDING THE *INTERSECTIONS* OF DIFFERENCE

Kimberlé Crenshaw (1989, 1991) is credited with introducing intersectionality in a critique of feminist studies, arguing that most feminist theory and studies made women of colour invisible, arguing that they were '...not subsumed within traditional boundaries of race or gender discrimination as these boundaries are currently understood' (1991: 1224). Intersectionality then refers to

> the interaction between gender, race and other categories of difference in the individual lives, social practices, institutional arrangements, and cultural ideologies and the outcomes of these interactions in terms of power. (Davis 2008: 68)

Since its 'arrival', it has been heralded, particularly within feminist studies, as one of the most important recent developments (Davis 2008; Walby et al. 2012). Much of the work that has followed has given central attention to the *intersection* between positions such as race, gender and class. The idea of 'triple oppression' (race, gender and class) where individual effects of sexism and racism are 'added up' has been called to be replaced with an approach that recognises a 'multiplicative effect within intersections' (McBride et al. 2015: 333) that exist *within* certain specific locations and experiences. So, for example, we must recognise that '...Black women experience sexism differently to that experienced by white women and experience racism in a different way to that of Black men' (McBride et al. 2015: 333). This is what Crenshaw (1991) calls 'structural intersectionality'.

While the notion of intersectionality has been widely accepted as a way of thinking outside traditional models around gender and race, it has been much debated (Davis 2008; McBride et al. 2015). One major criticism has been that, where the concept emerged out of debates within feminism over the relationship with the race question, there has been an ambivalence towards class (Walby et al. 2012). Walby et al. (2012) suggest that this is because class is not recognised as a justiciable inequality under EU legislation, where the legal and policy framework recognises gender, ethnicity, disability, age, religion/belief and sexuality as inequalities. Intersectionality has also found favour and success within post-structuralist and/or post-modernist theorising, particularly that it can make a significant contribution to 'diaspora studies' and 'queer theory' (Davis 2008). The latter, however, ignores that 'A queer identity may in fact only be accessible to those materially poised to occupy the position' (Taylor 2004: 4.1). Both New Zealand and Australia also have legislation that advocates for equality with the focus being on equal opportunity for all with attention on disadvantaged groups. For example, in Australia the Equality and Human Rights Commission[2] monitors human rights, protecting equality across nine grounds – age, disability, gender, race, religion and belief, pregnancy and maternity, marriage and civil partnership, sexual orientation and gender reassignment. Again similar to the UK/EU class is absent made. In this sense, it continued to advocate and encourage the movement away from class being seen as a core intersection. But we want to suggest that the work of Bourdieu can be invaluable in taking an intersectional approach.

Bourdieu and Intersectional Studies: Youth, Gender and Class

While intersectionality may lack some theoretical sophistication, it does create opportunities for feminist theorists to move beyond dualist or binary forms of analysis of class and gender that historically have remained unresolved and problematic (Adkins and Skeggs 2004; Davis 2008). Bourdieu's work offers an alternative framework that critically engages with the underlying structures of power and privilege that are, for us, the core business of intersectionality. While Bourdieu has been criticised for under theorising gender relationships (Moi 1991), his ideas have been since developed by both feminist and race theorists wanting to explore the intersections of gender and/or race and class in social relationships. In this context, it was proposed that gender should not be seen as a separate field, but that it ought to be conceptualised as a part of any field under investigation (Moi 1991). While interest in Bourdieu's work and gender has expanded, we will show there remains much to be done to advance this work further. First, it is important to note that a number of feminists have embraced the ideas of Bourdieu to explain how gender can and does operate in society:

> After reading Bourdieu I now feel confident that it is possible to link the humdrum details of everyday life to a more general social analysis of power. This in itself ought to make his approach attractive for feminists (Moi 1991)

Concepts such as 'habitus', 'field', 'cultural capital' and 'symbolic violence' are continually utilised in ways to illustrate how gender is socially constructed. Others have taken this further, arguing that Bourdieu's ideas are useful in understanding the relationship between gender and class. Probably the most renowned work is Skeggs (1997) book, *Formations of Class and Gender*, which provides a Bourdieusian analysis of the relationship between class and gender identities. Skeggs detailed ethnographic work with a group of working-class women in the UK shows how class and gender are fused together, and in doing so produces a detailed picture of the power relations such women encounter in modern society. While not 'naming' intersectionality, Skeggs explains how these women inhabited and occupied different social and cultural positions of class, gender and sexuality. Skeggs argued it was impossible to understand the everyday experiences of being a woman without recognising how such lives were structured, showing the marker of class as pivotal in their exclusion from the labour market, from the education system, from forms of cultural capital and from trading arenas. She also highlighted how working-class women were 'delegitimated through associations of non-respectability...' that created a '...emotional politics of class fuelled by insecurity, doubt, indignation and resentment.' This has a powerful impact on their lives in that it locked them into 'systems of self-regulation and monitoring, producing themselves as governable subjects' (1997: 162).

A second key contributor in the field was Diane Reay, who writing in 1997, responded to the growing 'class is dead thesis' generated by postmodernism to reassert the value of undertaking intersectional analyses of class and gender. Reay (1997: 225) argued that labour market relationships '...tell us very little about how social class processes are played out in social relationships'. Drawing on Bourdieu's concepts she showed how '...habitus enables us to understand women as complex amalgam of their past and present but an amalgam that is always in the process of completion' (1997: 227). She identifies how mothers rejected the identification of being working class seeing it, similar to those in Skeggs' study, as a form of 'social inferiority' (Reay 1997: 228). Reay proceeded to show how the social and economic position of working-class women coupled with the lack of cultural capital separates them from middle-class mothers:

> Those ingredients of cultural capital that the middle class women displayed; confidence, a sense of entitlement, knowledge of the educational system, useful social networks and a feeling of being capable of seizing the initiative are all absent.... (Reay 1997: 229)

In this sense, class and gender are clearly closely intertwined and connected. Thus, feminist studies offered a willingness to not only draw on the work of Bourdieu to examine the concept of gender but also its intersecting relationship with class and race. This was further advanced in the book *Feminism after Bourdieu*, edited by Adkins and Skeggs (2004); it is here where discussions about what Reay (2004) calls 'emotional capital' are introduced. This idea sees women take the burden or responsibility for emotional labour in the family and it is they who then pass this on to others as '... emotional capital is generally confined within the bounds of affective relationships of family and friends and encompasses the emotional resources you hand on to those you care about' (Reay 2004: 60).

A primary theoretical development emerging from this early feminist work has been the conceptualisation of 'gender' as a form of capital (Skeggs 1997; Lovell 2000; Huppatz 2010). Essentially to qualify as capital, a practice or cultural behaviour ought to be convertible in a way that has value within a social field that can then be deployed of one's advantage (or not). For example, Huppatz (2010) writing on the Australian care sector, teased out the classed nature of how gender capital can and does work in structuring the life trajectories and career pathways of women. More recently, this approach proposes the value of thinking about the interrelationship of both male and female forms of gender capital and how it impacts on life chances and opportunities of either men and/or women (Huppatz and Goodwin 2013). As Huppatz and Goodwin (2013: 297) state '... both femininity and masculinity are resources that are drawn on both consciously and unconsciously with varying success in movements through social space, particularly in the labour market'. From this position we can see not only how masculine and female forms of capital work to differentially position different genders in the labour market and between the public and private spheres, but also reveals how the same capital can be used to different effect according to one's own gender. Tellingly, Huppatz and Goodwin (2013: 304) note that the 'transgression of gender norms and the mobilisation of feminine capital can be so profitable it can sometimes assist men in moving class position', and that 'mobilisation of feminine embodiments may be particularly advantageous for working-class men who need to "halt losses" and find that most low-skilled employment opportunities in Australia are in service work'.

Yvette Taylor's (2010) edited collection *Classed Intersections: Spaces, Selves, Knowledges* also offers a range of chapters that seek to do justice to the significance of class as it intersects with multiple systems of difference and inequality, several of which use Bourdieu's thinking tools. Class, here, is considered in relation to gender and a variety of intersections such as sexuality, generation and practices around employment and parenting/motherhood, among others. One especially notable piece, by Evans (2010), highlights how class is lived not only through gender and race but also through family structures, all of which combine to produce a habitus that ensures young women's sense of self is bound to a sense of responsibility to 'become someone' for the sake of the wider family. Nonetheless, rather than needing to be re-worked in any dramatic sense, Bourdieu's own writing clarifies that gender is an important part of habitus, where he notes, for instance, that 'the classificatory schemes through which the body is apprehended and appreciated are always two fold, both in the social division of labour and in the sexual division of labour' (Bourdieu 1990: 72). Finally, echoing Skeggs, Allen (2014) illustrated how working-class women are often subjected to intensified scrutiny and portrayed as 'immoral' and not conveying the 'right' types of femininity. Each of these findings and pronouncements, rather than being a process of reinvention, in fact echo Bourdieu's subtle but implicit call to intersectionality. As Silva (2016) explains: 'It is important to note that in Bourdieu there is intersectionality and his analyses interweave complex modes of correspondence between sociality and fields. But for Bourdieu all factors such as age, gender, and ethnicity operate through the mechanism of a class-based habitus.' There are of course criticisms, and these often take aim at the lack of certainty of action that can now allegedly be read from class positions. However, again as Silva (2016) contends persuasively, 'The breaking down of the constituents of the structuring elements of social action requires a focused attention to field, since habitus operates in fields.' While she is promoting additions and developments for a more 'exciting' agenda for sociology (which we do not have space to detail here), Silva's remarks are a salutary reminder of the need to think through social action by employing Bourdieu *in toto* (see also Atkinson 2010, 2015).

INTERSECTIONAL STUDIES: YOUTH, GENDER AND CLASS

While feminism thought has enthusiastically engaged with Bourdieu's tools, his impact and influence, especially in youth studies, remains limited. In fact we would argue that work on *young* women and class virtually disappeared, especially in relation to girls in post-16 education and training and work (exceptions include Bowers-Brown 2015). Studies of youth and masculinity are rather different. Bourdieu's ideas initially offered limited insight into masculinities, at least explicitly. His most famous work in this area, *Masculine Domination* (2001), was chided by Connell and Messerschmidt (2005: 844) for giving 'a new lease of life to functionalism in gender studies'. This critique allies with others who have built their theories in ways that *appear* incommensurate with Bourdieu's ideas and rests in some ways on the perennial and, for us, (largely) misconstrued readings of Bourdieu's work as lacking in emphasis on agency and/or ability to account for change and transformation (Connell 1983; McLeod 2005; also Goldthorpe 2007). The critique of essentialism, especially, is mistaken. We concur with Dillabough (2004: 494) who makes this plain:

> [Bourdieu's] view of the performance of masculinity has an anti-essentialist character in that male domination can be traced to historical ideas that are embodied by social actors in the present. It is not simply a straightforward or objective derivative of contemporary social and cultural power formations. Arbitrary enactments of masculine domination are expressed and, therefore, to be read differently through social structures, discourses, relations and bodily representations.

Dillabough also uses Bourdieu's own words to again clarify just how ripe for analysis masculinity becomes through a Bourdieusian lens: 'as a man or women [...] we have embodied the historical structures of the masculine order in the form of unconscious schemes of perception and appreciation' (Bourdieu 2001: 5). Just how gender informs capitals and habitus, then, and indeed how this plays out, changes or endures is crucially important and something that studies of youth masculinity can sit comfortably with.

While relatively absent in Anglo literatures on masculinity, there has been a recent but slightly more long-standing trend in German-speaking literatures to combine theories of hegemonic masculinity and Bourdieusian conceptualisations to useful effect (Meuser 2009). Meuser (2009) explained how German-speaking sociologists readily align these two allegedly competing positions, using the Bourdieusian idea of masculine habitus to consider how individuals become *disposed* to acting according to, and thus incorporating, the given gender order and, complementarily, that starting from a position that sees masculinity as constructed within the serious games of competition played *among* men (Meuser 2009: 41). Meuser and Scholz (2005: 224–225) went further still, arguing powerfully that Bourdieu's analysis of masculine dominance, through highlighting incorporation, provides a better model than Connell in terms of explaining the persistence of established patterns of masculinity. This chimes well with a more sophisticated – but still middle ground – theoretical approach presented by Australian academic Tony Coles (2009) who argued that habitus, capitals and field permit better attention to how 'masculinity as an unconscious strategy forms part of the habitus of men that is both transposable and malleable to given situations to form practical dispositions and actions to everyday situations' (2009: 39). This more nuanced treatment of masculinity aids our understanding of how 'external sources of influence such as class, age, and ethnicity intersect with the field of masculinity to form complex matrices that allow for a variety of masculinities to exist' (Coles 2009: 38).

At the empirical level, Bourdieu-inflected readings of working-class young masculinities have recently emerged in English-language research. These studies, as in the recent German-speaking tradition, utilised Bourdieu to understand the existence of change alongside elements of persistence. For example, Stahl (2013) adopted neo-Bourdieusian ideas around institutional habitus to explore how working-class boys' learner identities are (sometimes problematically) restructured by attendance at a high-performing school in a socially marginalised area, pointing to the role of institutions in transforming or producing a divided habitus. Similarly, even while finding a distancing from older restricted codes of gender expression among elite-level, young, professional footballers, Roberts et al. (2016) emphasised the enduring nature of the football club's institutional habitus. Here, Bourdieu is used to explain why behaviours change as young men traverse their home locality and the 'football locality's' mandated, limited forms of emotional expression. In a similar vein, McCormack (2014) employs Bourdieu more fully by considering how habitus and capitals interlock to produce classed differences around embracing certain types of tactility. For McCormack, Bourdieu's symbolic economy is influential in producing relatively conservative levels of tactility among working-class teenagers, yet simultaneously working-class culture is not presented as being in deficit or pathological. Using capitals as to help understand *intra* generational difference, he also shows how differences in the production of habitus can explain *intergenerational* difference in expressions of masculinity. Finally, a coherent Bourdieusian theoretical approach was adopted by Thorpe (2010: 202), who, in her study of (young adult) snow boarders, notes how 'men's snowboarding identities, behaviours, and interactions (with other men and women) often change as they age and enter new life stages and gain (or lose) access to particular forms of capital (e.g., physical, symbolic, masculine, economic)'. Informed by a gendered reading of what she describes as the habitus–field complex, Thorpe illustrates 'how men's movement across, and within, social fields can prompt critical reflection on masculine practices and performances within the snowboarding culture as well as gender norms and values in other social fields'.

Bourdieu and Intersectional Studies: Youth, Race and Class

In terms of race and class, there is considerable amounts of research using, for example, attainment statistics that examines this intersection (e.g. Strand 2011; Berrington et al. 2016), but we limit our discussion to research explicitly concerned with the lived experience of race and class. Bourdieu has been criticised for his limited writing on the 'race question', with some arguing that this 'gap' extends to his failure to critically engage with the processes of colonialism in a detailed and systematic way (Connell 2007). Others have suggested that Bourdieu's concepts of cultural and social capital create the assumption that '...People of Color 'lack' the social and cultural capital required for social mobility...' (Yosso 2005). More recently, though, scholars working within a Bourdieusian framework have argued that Bourdieu's concepts can aid explanations of the interplay between race and class.

First, readers should consult Puwar's sensitive and well-informed article highlighting not only how 'the colonial and post-colonial presence in the historical practice of [Bourdieu's] intellectual explorations has not been centred in the communication of his intellectual corpus in lecture theatres' (2009: 373), but also that, and crucially, 'Attention to colonial legacies, sensitivity to cultural and epistemic violence, the demands and opportunities of migration, as well as the ambivalence of not belonging in legal and social registers – are all themes that Bourdieu worked on' (Puwar 2009: 373). Wallace (2016) similarly suggests the aforementioned negative perspectives on Bourdieu arise from limited readings and a failure to consider some less-known work. Race mattered to Bourdieu: he rejected fixed biographical categories that were dominant at his time of writing, being more interested in how Algeria constructed a caste system that created divisions between Europeans and Arabs, where the two 'societies' 'are placed in a relation of superior to inferior....' In this context, racism in Algeria was seen to '...provide a rationalisation of the existing state of affairs so as to make it appear to be lawfully instituted order' (Bourdieu 1962: 132 quoted by Wallace 2016). What Bourdieu suggested is that colonialism, through its creation of a caste system, not only helped reproduce social divisions but also provided various justifications and normative lawful frameworks. While Bourdieu emphasised caste as 'race' plus political privilege, he still observed strong connections between race and class seeing that each caste could be divided into classes that have clear boundaries that limit social mobility. Such a position suggests that 'caste functioned...as a definitive feature of class and colonial conditions', and that in the 'colonial order, structural racism and class inequality are deeply interconnected' (Wallace 2016: XX). Similarly, Bourdieu's later work on Brazil was highly critical of 'ethnocentric intrusion' that separates race from class analysis; he insisted that racial identity in Brazil can only be defined by first recognising a person's class position (Bourdieu and Wacquant 1999: 45).

Rollock et al. (2011, 2015), Wallace (2016) and others (Ball et al. 2002; Shah et al. 2010) promote extending developing the Bourdieusian toolbox to provide proper recognition to racialised processes, especially when looking at the intersections between class and race. As we will see, it is again in the field of the sociology of education where much of this work has evolved. A youth sociological analysis of how different ethnic young people experience the classed nature of labour markets and higher education has remained marginal. We believe that real opportunities exist for youth sociology to use a Bourdieusian approach to further illuminate these relations.

Playing the 'Middle Class Game'

In addressing intersecting axes of difference, we must acknowledge a growing middle class amongst some ethnic groups. Such growth has been explored through a Bourdieusian framework, asking how middle-class African Caribbean young people and their families operate in the largely white middle-class world in the UK (Rollock et al. 2011). While the analysis focuses on relations within compulsory schooling, it shows the importance of how young people and parents use 'language' and 'performance' to succeed in the middle-class white world, that is forms of embodied cultural capital, of different cultural styles, language and personas that are *recognisable* as middle class. 'Speaking properly' (not using street language such as Patois) and walking in certain ways is recognised as a way of signalling middle-class status. As a result, '... they are able to facilitate the creation of an invisible demarcation between themselves as middle class and other black people who are from working class backgrounds (Rollock et al. 2011: 1086). 'Sounding Black' is rejected and, using a middle-class accent as a 'signifier of middle class status', they actively minimise the chances that of discrimination on the basis of race. In these practices, young people and their parents actively engage in both 'exclusionary and inclusionary' boundary work – explicit efforts at making others aware of the class to which they do and do not belong (Rollock et al. 2011: 1087). Rollock et al. (2015) also identified the different ways that black middle-class parents deploy class resources and high status cultural codes to help them and their children become socially mobile. Again, cultural capital, in the form of academic qualifications alongside core middle-class dispositions, is mobilised to help children navigate their the education system. That said, the black middle-classes encounter 'advantage' in ways that differ significantly from their white counterparts. Race and racism, and not being 'white', can and does operate at different points to constrain both the experiences and usefulness of cultural capital.

Wallace (2016) developed the idea of 'black cultural capital', where young black Caribbean boys and their parents are strategic in mobilising traditional forms of cultural capital, using it to plan and reflect on how they should interact in the school setting. Young people continually reflect on the quality of their interactions, ensuring that they perform certain types of dispositions that are clearly visible and recognisable to their middle-class teachers. This 'playing the game' holds positive effects in that shared interactional codes, aesthetics, knowledges and speech styles that help them forge relationships with teachers who then help advance their careers. As part of this process, young people also mobilise a 'black' form of cultural capital that challenges the negative stigmatisation of black culture and enables them to assert a more positive form of cultural capital. Teachers are able to intersect aspects of black history, thus '...the intentional integration of black history marks attempts by black middle-class pupils to de-code and re-code dominant cultural capital to better reflect their racial background as class subjects' (Wallace 2016: 9). Such action is well received by white middle-class teachers, who often want to appear inclusive and racially aware. In this context, black history and certain types of cultural forms that reflect those interests of white middle-class teachers allow black students' cultural capital to be better recognised. Such practices are not without problems, creating tensions and difficulties sometimes re-enforce a distinction between 'low' and 'high' culture within their own social racialised groups. While teachers give recognition and respect to the use of examples from art, literature and music, their strategic use of such black capital 'positions' does not acknowledge that their access to and use of 'high culture' is partly facilitated by their parents' economic resources. Wallace's (2016) young participants were also cognisant of what he calls being 'multi-class minded', suggesting they recognise what separates them from young black people in poor areas is class differences and privilege, not race.

RACE AND CLASS IN HIGHER EDUCATION

Early research on exploring minority ethnic youth's involvement with higher education drew upon the work of Bourdieu, showing how race and class informed choice of university (Archer and Hutchings 2000; Ball et al 2002; Reay et al. 2005), providing good examples of how Bourdieu's tools permit analysis of this intersectional relationship. As per Chapter 3, a strong correlation exists between social class and higher education participation. Inserting race into the class theme raises interesting questions. For example, studies by Archer and Hutchings (2000) and Reay et al. (2005) found strong overlapping experiences of entering and exiting higher education for ethnically diverse young working-class respondents. These authors showed how being working class, regardless of ethnicity, was a major feature of young people's experience. This said, a number of racialised features existed that brought added stresses and difficulties for those from various minority ethnic backgrounds. While presuming their class background positioned them as ill-fitting for some of the most elite institutions, ethnic minority young people were further influenced in their decisions because '...the continued dominance of particular (elite) institutions by white people can work to render these institutions as 'unthinkable' choices for ethnic minority applicants' (Archer and Hutchings 2000: 563). Bourdieu would see this as the creation of a class distance where one's working-class habitus is mismatched and one's capitals are not convertible (Bourdieu and Passeron 1979); yet, for BME young people there appears to be an additional 'ethnic distance' which increases anxiety and uncertainty about selecting elite universities. There is, thus, a need for these young people to find an 'academic culture' and setting or location where they can connect with students from their 'own' social and ethnic strata (Reay et al. 2005). Consequently, many BME young people apply to universities that reflect not only their social class position but also their ethnicity. Evidence from the UK supports this, observing high concentrations of BME groupings in certain 'new' universities, particularly around London (HEFCE 2015). Yet, as we saw earlier, evidence in the UK also suggests that the active engagement in higher education of these groups varies by ethnicity and a simple reading of race and class is complicated. For example,

> While South Asians as a group had the highest rates of participation in post-compulsory education for the 16–24 age range, Indian and African-Asian men were the most likely to possess degrees and Pakistani and Bangladeshi men were the least likely. However, if young Pakistani men do less well than some of their South Asian peers, both young Pakistani men and women are more likely to go to university than their white peers. (Shah et al. 2010: 1110)

How can these trends be explained, especially in terms of relations to a young person's class position? Similar to Wallace's notion of 'black capital', Shah et al. (2010) suggest that there exists a form of 'ethnic capital' that operates to ameliorate or augment social class disadvantage. Building on Bourdieusian ideas, they suggest that there are missing links in his work on ethnicity, which fail to grasp the complex ways that structural position and location (i.e. being immigrants) impact on values and approaches towards education and work. Ethnic capital, then, includes not only cultural and social capital (family norms, values) but also social networks which can and do promote and support a particular set of educational values. In this context, Shah et al. (2010) suggest that many ethnic minority families bring with them values different to their objective class position in the country of destination. They exemplify this through consideration of British Pakistani families, who lack economic capital but hold values (and capitals) that would, in a British context, be presumed middle class. This is a form of transnational capital (Ball et al., 2002) established as a part of their habitus in Pakistan. This said, Shah et al. (2010) recognise that it may not neutralise all the effects of class disadvantages. It is also unclear to us how it addresses power inequalities *within* ethnic communities.

BOURDIEU, CLASS AND INDIGENOUS POPULATIONS

Our discussion has hitherto focussed on BME groups' experience of education in the UK. This is partly a result of the limited use of Bourdieu's ideas in Australia and New Zealand (Bennett et al. 2013) but also because, as we showed, his ideas have not held such traction outside the educational context, especially in relation to the questions of class and race. As we outlined in Chapter 2, Bourdieu's influence in the antipodes has been 'patchy', and, when it comes to wider questions of class, his influence has been almost non-existent (Woodward and Emmison 2009). This limited influence, in no small part, stems from an *incorrect* assessment that Bourdieu's theory is Eurocentric (Connell 2007) and lacks any real appreciation of colonialism (Said 1989). Julian Go (2013) provides an excellent, highly detailed account of what Bourdieu brings to colonial studies to counter this.

Bourdieu's work has begun to influence issues around indigenous culture (Myers 2013: McCarthy 2013), but this often focuses on debates related to Bourdieu's work on distinction and cultural practice. We suggest that one of the more interesting possibilities for using of Bourdieu is in explaining the specific experience of indigenous populations, namely that of New Zealand Māori and Aboriginal and Torres Strait people in Australia. Bourdieu has, indeed, been criticised for offering a 'Northern theory' that operates within a particular liberal modern framework and which gives little recognition to how colonising experiences have marginalised and ignored indigenous worldviews (Connell 2007). Yet, Bourdieu *could* make a major contribution to this area.

The immediate point to highlight is that, while class is seen as having little value in New Zealand and Australia, both New Zealand Māori and

Australian Aboriginal and Torres Strait people are predominantly located in the bottom three SES groups. For example, historically New Zealand Māori have been far behind European New Zealanders in terms of wealth ownership and income levels, but since the 1980s they have fallen even further behind. The neoliberal policy agenda has restructured financial and labour markets in ways that favour the rich and privileged (Poata-Smith 2013), such that ranking New Zealand households from the poorest 20% (quintile one) to the richest 20% (quintile five) consistently shows households with a Māori adult as disproportionately represented amongst the first three quintiles, and significantly under-represented amongst those on high incomes (Poata-Smith 2013: 151) This is significant because, simultaneously, real incomes of the bottom 60% throughout this period declined, while those in the top 20% increased. While the policies of New Zealand's Labour government of 2000–2008 reduced inequality slightly, it has since been rising (France 2016). Similar patterns exist in Australia, where wealth and income inequality remains high and where indigenous people are hit hardest. For example, just 13% of Aboriginal and Torres Strait Islander people have a gross income of AUS$1000 per week compared to 33% of the non-indigenous population. In terms of wealth ownership, Aboriginal and Torres Strait Islander people are firmly located in the bottom quintile (Commonwealth of Australia 2014).

Poata-Smith (2004) suggested that most New Zealanders see the position of Māori as a result of colonialism, but argues that class interests are critical to these discussions. While successive governments in New Zealand have established a settlement framework for past injustices, this framework '…locks Māori self-determination into a free-market, capitalist economic framework…' (Poata-Smith 2004: 60), which has emphasised and promoted a strategy of commercial development that denies and rejects more radical alternatives. Furthermore, it also privileges the commercial wing of *iwi* to negotiate, not only claims but also distribution of resources and '…concentrates decision-making power in the hands of full-time tribal executives who have objective interests in the profitability of tribal commercial ventures…' (61). This in effect increases inequality and creates class divisions within Māori *iwi* (Poata-Smith 2004). While this contributes to class divisions, neoliberal reform and the growing social inequalities have also not affected all Māori equally. Māori are not entirely excluded from the middle class, with recent evidence showing some Māori families are located in the top quintile (fifth) in terms of income, and small numbers of Māori have increased their share of wealth

(Poata-Smith 2013: 151). Similar to New Zealand there is also a growing middle class that are emerging partly because of growing numbers of professional workers, increasing by 74% between 1996 and 2006. These jobs, for Māori, tend to be in education, visual arts, environmental science and human resources (Lahn 2013).

So, in terms of economic capital, the vast majority of New Zealand Māori and Aboriginal and Torres Strait Islander people in Australia are still located at the bottom of the class structure. But *how* class operates to shape young indigenous groups' opportunities and outcomes remain unclear. We believe that by introducing a Bourdieusian approach, the complexity of this relationship could be further untangled and explained. For example, in New Zealand, traditionally the Māori way of life was distinctively different from that of their colonisers (Bartley and Spoonley 1999) and while colonisation attempted to erase Māori way of life, much still remains today. A good example of this is *Te Reo*, the Māori language. During colonising process it was almost totally destroyed. In the 1980s, however, it gained greater influence; although it is still a minority spoken language, it is now recognised as a language of New Zealand (along with English and Sign language) and is part of the national curriculum in the education system and has state support. In fact, what can be seen is that Māori ideas and life world theories are gaining stronger influence on public and social policy (Smith 1999). This is partly as a result of the New Zealand State recognising and officially promoting (to some extent) bi-culturalism and tacking the injustices that were done under the practice of colonialism. What is clear, then, is that Māori culture and practice still exists, although its influence and 'shaping qualities' especially on the young will and do vary. While many of the traditional practices and structures of Māori remain, the context in which young Māori live in New Zealand has now changed substantially and its role and influence both in practice and at the level of ideas can and does vary across different 'fields'. For example, young Māori are more likely to live in urban centres where Māori culture and ways of living can appear to hold less relevance (Edwards et al. 2007).

Using a Bourdieusian approach to the dispositions of habitus for young Māori can and would better emphasise the influences of their encounters in social space, and in their childhood of Māori culture and ideas. While we would be cautious about the idea of a Māori habitus (given our points earlier), we do believe that investigating the interplay between young people's Māori up-bringing and the modern liberal capitalist that is now dominant in New Zealand creates a particular habitus and experience of growing up. We also believe that similar to the idea of 'black capitals' or 'ethnic' capitals discussed earlier, a form of 'Brown[3]' (or Māori) capital could be a useful way of thinking about how cultural and social capitals might work in New Zealand. For example, Māori culture has hierarchical structures and protocols and your 'position' in the hapū and iwi alongside your 'mana' and tribal history seems, we believe, to create a particular form of capital which can give greater influence. But capitals are valuable only in relation to certain fields. As Bourdieu reminds us (and we continually show), fields are critical spaces for capitals to give people advantage and opportunities. Importantly here, (post) colonialism can be understood as a system with its own logic, that is like a field in its own right, characterised by contrasting communities of dominant and subordinate, but in this case colonised and colonisers (Go 2013). Understanding indigenous young people's habitus and capitals, then, can be effectively realised through the relational tools that Bourdieu offers. This will aid the development of a more holistic view of their marginalisation and domination.

Conclusion

Given our discussion previously, we believe that class needs to be reinstituted as a central feature to the analysis of other inequalities. Its relative marginalisation in the study of gender and race reduces the impact of more structural features and denies the ways that differences and inequalities are further mediated/exacerbated by class. As writers in feminist and race studies have shown, a Bourdieusian analysis of gender and race can be enhanced by showing the intersections of these inequalities. Intersectionality, we feel is especially relevant to youth sociology. While historically class was always assumed in many discussions about gender and race, it has virtually disappeared partly by design (i.e. post-structuralism) and partly by a desire to illuminate the distinctive nature of gender or racial relationships (i.e. the growth of identity studies), but we suggest that reinserting class inequality into the analysis will create a better understanding of how the lives of young women and different ethnic groups are being shaped. Finally, again we want to highlight the importance of how these experiences of class are framed and contextualised by the fields in which young people have to operate. Understanding these through a broader lens is, as we have suggested, critical. For example, historical immigration in the UK, colonialism in Australia and New Zealand alongside the expansion of neoliberalist policy and practice are critical in structuring the fields that ethnic or indigenous young people encounter in different national settings. Fields are clearly places of struggles, but their rules and practices are also strongly influenced by broad historical and global process.

Notes

1. Data from Statisics New Zealand website http://www.stats.govt.nz/browse_for_stats/snapshots-of-nz/yearbook/society/crime/corrections.aspx
2. This was established in 1986 as the Human Rights and Equal Opportunity Commission and renamed in 2008. It is a statutory body funded by, but operating independently of, the Australian Government.
3. 'Brown' is a term used in New Zealand to represent people from the Polynesian cultures.

References

Aapola, S., Gonick, M., & Harris, A. (2005). *Young femininity: Girlhood, power, and social change*. London: Palgrave Macmillan.

Adkins, L., & Skeggs, B. (Ed.) (2004). *Feminism after Bourdieu*. Oxford: Blackwell Publishing.

Allen, K. (2014). 'Blair's children': Young women as 'aspirational subjects' in the psychic landscape of class. *The Sociological Review*, 62(4), 760–779.

Archer, L. (2003). *Race, masculinity and schooling: Muslim boys and education*. UK: McGraw-Hill Education.

Archer, L., & Hutchings, M. (2000). 'Bettering Yourself'? Discourses of risk, cost and benefit in ethnically diverse, young working-class non-participants' constructions of higher education. *British Journal of Sociology of Education*, 21(4), 555–574.

Archer, L., & Yamashita, H. (2003). Theorising inner-city masculinities: 'Race', class, gender and education. *Gender and Education*, 15(2), 115–132.

Atkinson, W. (2010). The myth of the reflexive worker: Class and work histories in neo-liberal times. *Work, Employment and Society*, 24(3), 413–429.

Atkinson, W. (2015). *Class*. Cambridge: Polity Press.

Ball, S. J., Davies, J., David, M., & Reay, D. (2002). 'Classification' and 'Judgement': Social Class and the 'Cognitive Structures' of Choice of Higher Education. *British journal of sociology of education*, 23(1), 51–72.

Barone, C. (2011). Somethings never change: Gender segregation in higher education across eight nations and three decades. *Sociology of Education*, *84*(2), 157–176.
Bartley, A., & Spoonley, P. (1999). Constructing a Workable Multiculturalism in a Bicultural Siociety. In Fleras, A. and Spoonley, P. (Eds.), *Recalling Aotearoa: Indigenous Politics and Ethnic Relations in New Zealand*. Oxford: Oxford University Press.
Bates, I. (1993a). A job which is 'right for me'. In I. Bates & G. Riseborough (Ed.), *Youth and inequality*. Buckingham: Open University.
Bates, I. (1993b). When I get my own Studio. In I. Bates & G. Riseborough (Ed.), *Youth and inequality*. Buckingham: Open University Press.
Bennett, T., Frow, J., Hage, G., & Noble, G. (2013). Antipodean fields. *Journal of Sociology*, *49*(2–3), 129–150.
Berrington, A., Roberts, S., & Tammes, P. (2016). Educational aspirations among UK young teenagers: Exploring the role of gender, class and ethnicity. *British Educational Research Journal*, *42*(5), 729–755.
Bourdieu, P. (1962). *The Algerians*. Boston: Beacon Press.
Bourdieu, P. (1990). *The Logic of Practice*. Cambridge: Polity Press.
Bourdieu, P. (2001). *Masculine domination*. California: Stanford University Press.
Bourdieu, P., & Passeron, J. C. (1979). *The inheritors: French students and their relation to culture*. London: Chicago University Press.
Bourdieu, P., & Wacquant, L. (1999). On the cunning of imperialist reason. *Theory, Culture and Society*, *16*(1), 41–58.
Bowers-Brown, T. (2015). It's like if you don't go to Uni you fail in life. *Bourdieu: The Next Generation: The Development of Bourdieu's Intellectual Heritage in Contemporary UK Sociology*, 55.
Brynin, M., & Longhi, S. (2015). *The effect of occupation on poverty among ethnic minority groups*. York: JRF.
Burt, C. (1925). *The Young Delinquent*. London: University of London Press.
Catney, G., & Sabater, A. (2015). *Ethnic minority disadvantage in the labour market*. York: JRF.
Coles, T. (2009). Negotiating the field of masculinity; The production and reproduction of multiple dominant masculinities. *Men and Masculinities*, *12*(1), 30–44.
Commonwealth of Australia. (2014). *Bridging our growing divide: inequality in Australia: The extent of income inequality in Australia*. Canberra: Commonwealth of Australia.
Connell, R. (1983). Social Class in Australia. *Search*, *14*, 247–248.
Connell, R. (2005). *Masculinities*. Cambridge: Polity Press.
Connell, R. (2007). *Southern theory: The global dynamics of knowledge in social science*. NSW, Australia: Allen and Unwin.

Connell, R. W., & Messerschmidt, J. W. (2005). Hegemonic masculinity rethinking the concept. *Gender and Society, 19*(6), 829–859.

Crawford, C., & Greaves, E. (2015). *Socio-economic, ethnic and gender differences in HE participation*. Report 186. London: Department for Business, Innovation and Skills.

Crenshaw, K. W. (1989). Demarginalizing the intersection of race and sex: A black feminist critique of antidiscrimination doctrine, feminist theory, and anti-racist policies. *Legal Forum, 14*, 538–554.

Crenshaw, K. W. (1991). Mapping the margins: Intersectionality, identity politics and violence against women of color. *Stanford Law Review, 43*(6), 1241–1299.

Davis, K. (2008). Intersectionality as buzzword: A sociology of science perspective on what makes a feminist theory successful. *Feminist Theory, 9*(1), 67–85.

Dillabough, J. A. (2004). Class, culture and the 'predicaments of masculine domination': Encountering Pierre Bourdieu. *British Journal of Sociology of Education, 25*(4), 489–506.

Edwards, S., McCreanor, T., & Moewaka-Barnes, H. (2007). Maori family culture: A context of youth development in Counties/Manukau. *Kōtuitui: New Zealand Journal of Social Sciences Online, 2*(1), 1–15.

Equity Challenge Unit. (2013). *Equality in higher education: statistical report*. London: Equality Challenge Unit.

Evans, S. (2010). Becoming 'Somebody': Examining class and gender through higher education. In Y. Taylor (Ed.), *Classed intersections: Space, selves and knowledges*. London: Routledge.

Finn, D. (1987). *Training without jobs: New deals and broken promises*. London: Macmillan Education.

Fong, B., & Phelps, A. (2007). *Apprenticeship Pay: 2007 Survey of Earnings by Sector*. Research Report 08–05. London: Department for Innovation, Universities and Skills.

France, A. (2007). *Understanding youth in late modernity*. Buckingham: Open University Press.

France, A. (2016). *Understanding youth in the global economic crisis*. Bristol: Policy Press.

Francis, B. (1999). Lads, lasses and (new) labour: 14–16-year-old students' responses to the 'laddish behaviour and boys' underachievement' debate. *British Journal of Sociology of Education, 20*(3), 355–371.

Gilroy, P. (1987). *There ain't no black in the Union Jack*. London: Hutchinson.

Go, J. (2013). Decolonizing Bourdieu: Colonial and postcolonial theory in Pierre Bourdieu's early work. *Sociological Theory, 31*(1), 49–74.

Goldthorpe, J. H. (2007). "Cultural Capital": Some critical observations. *Acta Sociologica, 50*(3), 211–229.

Gorden, L. (2015). Teaching the 'Poor' a lesson: Beyond punitive discipline in schools. *New Zealand Journal of Educational Studies, 50*(2), 211–222.

Griffin, C. (1985). *Typical girls? Young women from school to the job market.* London: Routledge and Kegan Paul London.

Griffin, C. (1993). *Representations of Youth: The study of youth and adolescence in Britain and America.* Cambridge: Polity Press.

Griffin, C. E. (2011). The trouble with class: Researching youth, class and culture beyond the 'Birmingham School'. *Journal of Youth Studies, 14*(3), 245–259.

Harris, A. (2004). *Future girl: Young women in the Twenty First Century.* New York: Routledge.

Heath, A., & Cheung, S. Y. (2007) *Ethnic penalties in the labour market: employers and discrimination.* Report No. 341 London: Department for Work and Pensions.

Hebdige, D. (1979). *Subculture: The Meaning of Style.* London: Methuen & Co.

HEFCE. (2015). *Differences in employment outcomes; Equality and diversity characteristics.* London: Higher Education Funding Council for England.

Hollands, R. G. (1990). *The long transition: Class, culture and youth training.* London: Macmillan Education.

Hopkins, P. E. (2006). Youthful Muslim masculinities: Gender and generational relations. *Transactions of the Institute of British Geographers, 31*(3), 337–352.

Hudson, M., Netto, G., Sosenko, F., Noon, M., De Lima, P., Gilchrist, A., & Kamenou-Aigbekaen, N. (2013). *In work poverty, ethnicity and workplace cultures.* York: JRF.

Huppatz, K. (2010). Class and career choice: Motivations, aspirations, identity and mobility for women in paid caring work. *Journal of Sociology, 46*(2), 115–132.

Huppatz, K., & Goodwin, S. (2013). Masculinised jobs, feminised jobs and men's 'gender capital' experiences: Understanding occupational segregation in Australia. *Journal of Sociology, 49*(2–3), 291–308.

Ingram, N. (2009). Working-class boys, educational success and the misrecognition of working-class culture. *British Journal of Sociology of Education, 30*(4), 421–434.

Lahn, L. (2013). *Aboriginal professional: work, class and culture.* 89/2013. Canberra: Australian National University.

Lancrin, V. (2008). *The reversal of gender inequalities in higher education: The ongoing trends in OECD, higher education trends to 2030.* Paris: OECD.

Lea, J., & Young, J. (1984). *What is to be done about: Law and order?.* Penguin: Harmondsworth.

Lovell, T. (2000). Thinking feminism with and against Bourdieu. In B. Fowler (Ed.), *Reading Bourdieu on society and culture.* Blackwell: Oxford.

Low Pay Commission. (2014). *The national minimum wage.* CM8816. London: Department for Business and Innovation.

Marriot, L., & Sim, D. (2015). Indicators of inequality for Māori and Pacific people. *Journal of New Zealand Studies, 20*, 24–50.

McBride, A., Hebson, G., & Holgate, J. (2015). Intersectionality: Are we taking enough notice in the field of work and employment. *Work, Employment and Society*, 29(2), 331–341.

McCarthy, C. (2013). The rules of (Maori) art: Bourdieu's cultural sociology and Maori visitors in New Zealand museums. *Journal of Sociology*, 49(2–3), 173–193.

McCormack, M. (2014). The intersection of youth masculinities, decreasing homophobia and class: An ethnography. *The British Journal of Sociology*, 65(1), 130–149.

McDowell, L. (2003). *Redundant masculinities? Employment change and white working class youth*. Oxford: Wiley – Blackwell.

McDowell, L. (2012). Post-crisis, post-Ford and post-gender? Youth identities in an era of austerity. *Journal of Youth Studies*, 15(5), 573–590.

McLeod, J. (2005). Feminists re-reading Bourdieu old debates and new questions about gender habitus and gender change. *Theory and Research in Education*, 3(1), 11–30.

McRobbie, A. (1978). Working Class Girls and Femininity. *Women's Studies Group (CCCS), Women Take Issue. Aspect of Women's Subordination, Birmingham,*

Meer, N., & Nayak, A. (2015). Race ends where? Race, racism and contemporary sociology. *Sociology*, 49(6), NP3–NP20.

Meuser, M. (2009). Research on masculinities in German-Speaking countries: Developments, discussions and research themes. *Culture, Society and Masculinities*, 1(1), 33.

Meuser, M., & Scholz, S. (2005). Hegemoniale Männlichkeit—Versuch einer Begriffs- klärung aus soziologischer Perspektive [Hegemonic masculinity—attempt to clarify the concept from a sociological perspective]. In M. Dinges (Ed.), Männer—Macht— Körper. Hegemoniale Männlichkeiten vom Mittelalter bis heute (pp. 211–228). Frankfurt a.M.: Campus.

Moi, T. (1991). Appropriating Bourdieu: Feminist theory and Pierre Bourdieu's society of culture. *New Literary History*, 22(4), 1017–1049.

Myers, F. (2013). Disturbances in the field: Exhibiting aboriginal art in the US. *Journal of Sociology*, 49(2–3), 151–172.

Nava, M., & Nava, O. (1992). Discriminating of duped? Young people as consumers of advertising. In M. Nava (Ed.), *Changing cultures: Feminism, youth and consumption*. London: Sage.

Nayak, A. (2003). Last of the 'Real Geordies'? White masculinities and the subcultural response to deindustrialisation. *Environment and Planning D: Society and Space*, 21(1), 7–25.

Nixon, D. (2009). I Can't Put a Smiley Face On': Working-Class masculinity, emotional labour and service work in the 'New Economy'. *Gender, Work and Organization*, 16(3), 300–322.

O'Donnell, M., & Sharpe, S. (2002). *Uncertain masculinities: Youth, ethnicity, and class in contemporary Britain*. London: Psychology Press.

Poata-Smith, E. (2004). Ka Tika A Muri, Ka Tika A Mua? Maori Protest Politics and the Treaty of Waitangi Settlement. In P. Spoonley, Macpherson, & D. Pearson (Ed.), *Tanata Tangata: The changing ethnic contours of New Zealand*. Southbank, Victoria: Dunmore Press.

Poata-Smith, E. (2013). Inequality and Maori. In M. Rashbrooke (Ed.), *Inequality: A New Zealand crisis*. Wellington: Bridget Williams Books.

Puwar, N. (2009). Sensing a post-colonial Bourdieu: An introduction. *The Sociological Review, 57*(3), 371–384.

Reay, D. (1997). Feminist theory, habitus and social class: Disrupting notions of classlessness. *Women's Studies International Forum, 20*(2), 225–233.

Reay, D. (2004). Gendering Bourdieu's concept of capitals? Emotional capital, women and social class. In L. Adkins & B. Skeggs (Ed.), *Feminism after Bourdieu*. Oxford: Blackwell Publishers.

Reay, D., David, M., & Ball, S. (2005). *Degrees of choice: Social class, race and gender in higher education*. Stoke on Trent: Trentham Books.

Roberts, S. (2013). Boys will be boys…won't they? Change and continuities in contemporary young working-class masculinities. *Sociology, 47*(4), 671–686.

Roberts, S. (Ed.) (2014). *Debating modern masculinities: Change, continuity, crisis?*. Berlin: Springer.

Roberts, S., Anderson, E., & Magrath, R. (2016). Continuity, change and complexity in the performance of masculinity among elite young footballers in England. *The British Journal of Sociology*, 1–16.

Roberts, K., Clark, S. C., & Wallace, C. (1994). Flexibility and Individualisation: A Comparison of Transitions into Employment in England and Germany. *Sociology, 28*(1), 31–54.

Rollock, N., Gillborn, D., Vincent, C., & Ball, S. (2011). The public identities of the black middle classes: Managing race in public spaces. *Sociology, 45*(6), 1078–1093.

Rollock, N., Gillborn, D., Vincent, C., & Ball, S. (2015). *The colour of class: The educational strategies of the black middle classes*. Abington: Routledge.

Said, E. (1989). Representing the colonized: Anthropology's interloctors. *Critical Inquiry, 15*(2), 205–225.

Scarman, L. J. (1981). *The Brixton disorders, 10–12th April (1981)*. London: HMSO.

Shah, B., Dwyer, C., & Modood, T. (2010). Explaining educational achievement and career aspirations among young British Pakistanis: Mobilizing 'Ethnic Capital'? *Sociology, 44*(6), 1109–1127.

Shepherd, S. M., & Ilalio, T. (2016). Maori and Pacific Islander overrepresentation in the Australian criminal justice system—what are the determinants? *Journal of Offender Rehabilitation, 55*(2), 113–128.

Silva, E. (2016). Habitus: Beyond sociology. *The Sociological Review, 64*(1), 73–92.

Skeggs, B. (1997). *Formations of class and gender: Becoming respectable*. London: Sage.
Smart, C. (1976). *Crime and criminology*. London: Routledge and Kegan Paul.
Smith, L. T. (1999). *Decolonizing methodologies*. Dunedin: University of Otago Press.
Stahl, G. (2013). Habitus disjunctures, reflexivity and white working-class boys' conceptions of status in learner and social identities. *Sociological Research Online, 18*(3), 2.
Strand, S. (2011). The limits of social class in explaining ethnic gaps in educational attainment. *British Educational Research Journal. 37*(2), 197–229.
Taylor, Y. (2004). Negotiation and navigation-an exploration of the spaces/places of working-class lesbians. *Sociological Research Online, 9*, 1.
Taylor, Y. (2010). *Classed intersections: spaces, selves and knowledges*. London: Routledge.
Thornton, S. (1995). *Club cultures: Music, media and subcultural capital*. Cambridge: Polity Press.
Thorpe, H. (2010). Bourdieu, gender reflexivity, and physical culture: A case of masculinities in the snowboarding field. *Journal of Sport and Social Issues, 34*(2), 176–214.
TUC. (2014). *Living on the Margins: Black workers and casualisation*. London: Trade Union Congress.
Walby, S., Armstrong, J., & Sofia, S. (2012). Intersectionality: Multiple inequalities in social theory. *Sociology, 46*(2), 224–240.
Walkerdine, V., Lucey, H., & Melody, J. (2001). *Growing up Girl: Psycho-social explorations of gender and class*. London: Palgrave.
Wallace, D. (2016). Reading 'Race' in Bourdieu? Examining black cultural capital among black Caribbean youth in South London. *Sociology*.
Ward, M. R. (2015). *From labouring to learning: Working-class masculinities, education and de-industrialization*. Springer.
Willis, P. (1977). *Learning to labour: How working class kids get working class jobs*. Farnborough: Farnborough Saxon House.
Woodward, I., & Emmison, M. (2009). The intellectual reception of Bourdieu in Australian social sciences and humanities. *Sociological, 2*(3), 1–22.
Yosso, T. J. (2005). Whose culture has capital? A critical race theory discussion of community cultural wealth. *Race Ethnicity and Education, 8*(1), 69–91.

CHAPTER 6

Conclusion: Towards a New Agenda for Youth Sociology

Abstract Our intention has been to demonstrate that, even in so called new times, while the exact nature of social class inequalities has altered, they remain in familiar and enduring ways in the lives of young people. Here we briefly summarise our position regarding the significance of a Bourdieusian approach, contending that the youth research agenda needs to tackle the myths of classless societies, and expose such myths as what Bourdieu refers to as *doxa*. By rendering visible the arbitrariness of social arrangements, we can better illuminate youth as a period characterised by a relational struggle.

Keywords Youth · Class relations · Bourdieu · Doxa · Struggle

A Research Agenda for Youth Sociology?

Throughout the previous discussion our simple and clear message is that class has and continues to matter. By drawing on Bourdieu's scholarship, we have set about illuminating how, even in times of rapid social change, class remains influential for the young across a wide range of social fields. We advocate, following on from the work on social class and Bourdieu in mainstream sociology (Atkinson 2015; Savage 2015), that this approach needs to continue. As we have suggested elsewhere (France and Roberts 2015; France and Threadgold 2016; Roberts and France 2016; France 2017), those arguing for a political economy (see Cotê 2014) or social generational approach (see Woodman and Wyn 2015) tend to give limited attention to the divisions *within* or *across* generations. We have addressed these weaknesses by drawing the ideas of Bourdieu to show that we can only understand the 'lived experiences' of young people by recognising the important role that social divisions such as class has to play.

As we have seen in the previous discussions, there is a growing body of scholars in youth sociology that see the work of Bourdieu as critical and this work, we would argue, offers innovation and opportunities to understand the complex ways that class for the young is being maintained. By using a Bourdieusian lens, we are able to see the diverse and complex ways that class operates and how it is influential in shaping the 'lived experiences' of young people's lives in contemporary times. Along the way we have not wanted to devalue the importance of how other inequalities can and do operate in young people's lives. Work emphasising intersectionality shows us how we can create new ways of analysis that can bring together class with gender and/or race (and of course other dimensions of difference such as sexuality, disability etc.), ensuring a fuller explanation of how these inequalities combine or intersect to create diverse classed experiences.

While there is increasing interest in developing a Bourdieusian analysis of class in sociology (Savage 2015b), youth sociology has not always seized the opportunity to build on this in a coordinated or sustained way. As we saw, a Bourdieusian approach is a salient feature of much education research, with considerable use of Bourdieu's thinking tools in analysing social reproduction in schooling and, increasingly, post-16 training and higher education. This we believe is very important work and illuminates how young people's 'choices' and lived experiences of university structure their classed pathways and futures. However, more analysis is needed regarding how these processes operate in the vocational training sector and around the area of training apprenticeships. Historically, youth sociology had much to say about this field, showing how vocational training contributed to how working-class young people got working-class jobs (Bates et al. 1984). A return to this work using a Bourdieusian framework, we believe, would be invaluable.

While the sociology of education has made large strides in class analysis, we believe there is much to be done around young people's experiences of the labour market. It seems ironic to us that while youth sociology had a strong history of exploring the classed nature of work (e.g. Roberts 1995), in more recent times it has become marginal to the analysis of class. Issues of underemployment, precariousness and the possibility of a growing 'gig' economy have quite rightly dominated much of the recent analysis of young people's labour market relationships, but very little of this analysis gives attention to the classed nature of these processes. We strongly advocate that youth sociology address this gap around social class and work, which will, we believe, help make sense of who benefits (or not) from these developments and conditions.

Doxa and the 'Myth of Classlessness'

As we saw in the discussions about Australia and New Zealand, the notion of classlessness is embedded in a discourse and public imagination that claims these countries are fundamentally built on principles, suggesting they are 'meritocratic' or 'egalitarian' societies. Our discussions have aimed to challenge these claims, showing that not only does class exist in these two countries, but also that a Bourdieusian framework means class processes can be further illuminated. While in the UK class has stronger traction in public discourses, the public imagination of it is still greatly influenced by the notion that British society is 'open' and 'fluid' and that 'hard work' will allow people to move up the class structure. Bourdieu (1998a) has much to say about how and why these myths are perpetuated, most notably through the use of his concept of doxa. Doxa includes the self-evident, taken-for-granted articulations of reality: for example, social mobility can be achieved if one works hard enough, hence our material and symbolic status is a reflection of our effort in this fair society. This then relates to the unquestioned acceptance of the established order. As Bourdieu says, the established '...political order is perceived not as arbitrary...but as a self-evident and natural order which goes without saying and therefore goes unquestioned, the agents' aspirations have the same limits as the objective conditions of which they are a product' (Bourdieu 1977: 164). But not only this, but doxa also operates to maintain the social order as it is, while also imposing a structure of domination:

> Doxa is a particular point of view, the point of view of the dominant, which presents and imposes itself as a universal point of view – the point of view of those who dominate by dominating the state and who have constituted their point of view as universal by constituting the state (Bourdieu 1998b: 57)

The notion of classless societies are therefore important to the current doxa and are a part of the prevailing discourse of governments in countries such as Australia and New Zealand. Thus, the popular logic presented to citizens is that social mobility is a possibility that it does not matter where you come from, only where you are going and if you want to be successful you can do so. Differences in material and symbolic success is, thus, legitimated and misrecognised as a product of individual's own efforts or failures. Much sociology is geared towards exposing the doxa, and its maintenance through orthodoxy (the dominant defending how things are), and giving the possibility for challenging the status quo (heterodoxy). However, unlike, say, feminist-inspired accounts of the social world, in our view youth sociology does not do this so well. It lacks in theories of action for many inequalities and differences. For example, as well as establishing who is likely to be a NEET, we need to better theorise why *anyone* comes to be NEET, and why *particular* young people come to be a NEET and why some can navigate NEET status better than others. Bourdieu's sociology then provides the tools to do this and at the same time hold to account the powerful and expose the processes that lead to and maintain dominance. It can reveal the arbitrariness of social arrangements, where people's misrecognised 'perfect sense of limits' (Moi 1991: 1027) in relation to material and symbolic status and position in society, produced by the prevailing doxa, can be disrupted and transformed. Crucially, rather than see Bourdieu's as a sociology of determinism, instead it should be seen as stemming from a pessimism and frustration with the influence of doxa (Moi 1991); it is ultimately a sociology geared towards the possibility for transformation and of praxis.

We have also attempted to highlight the importance of how class operates in the antipodes and, while we recognise that further detailed analysis is required, we believe that Bourdieu has much to offer in these discussions. Some have previously argued that Bourdieu has limited value in understanding the lived experiences of people's living in the southern hemisphere (Connell 2007); this is a position we reject. We have showed, in Chapter 5, one way Bourdieu's work could be put to use, but we also think that concepts such as *doxa* offer an opportunity for us to understand how and why the notion of 'classlessness' is so influential in Australian and New Zealand thinking, especially in debates around the growing problem of inequality. We strongly believe there is an opportunity for us to draw upon the ideas of doxa to help better expose how class operates at the level of the 'invisible', while all the time having massive implications for the lived experiences of young people in the antipodes.

Of course much of our analysis in the previous chapters has highlighted the processes of social reproduction within this broader context of doxa. What we need to recognise is that within this, social reproduction can only be understood through the notion of struggle. As Threadgold reminds us,

> 'Bourdieu's approach to class embodies his relentlessly relational conception of social life' (Wacquant 2013: 275). While his approach has mostly been categorised towards understanding social reproduction, it is in fact the notion of struggle that is central to Bourdieu's work and key to understanding social reproduction and social change (Threadgold 2015)

This suggests that, in constructing a new class-focused research agenda for youth sociology, we need to adopt a *relational perspective* that embeds social action in a process of struggle. One area in particular that we should and can explore further relates to the notion of privilege and advantage. At various points throughout our exploration of key works, we found limited material on the activities of the rich and privileged. Exactly how social class privilege protects the interests of the elite within a massified higher education system and how it works in the graduate employment market is open to further empirical investigation. We would suggest that in focussing on one group (usually the most deprived or the 'problems of the proletariat', to quote Savage 2015) we produce only partial insights. A more relational approach, and more detailed research on, for example, how dominant groups use, reproduce and further accrue privilege is an essential part of understanding 'struggle' and for delivering the possibility of social change.

When thinking about the concept of struggle it is also important to recognise the much undertheorised workings of fields. As we have showed across the previous discussion fields are critical, not only to Bourdieu's thinking and approach but also to the 'lived experience' of young people. The field is a *specific* space that embodies struggles over perspectives, values, resources and legitimate ways of being. They are 'social microcosms' (Bourdieu 1998b: 138) that structure social formations and situations, particularly around the uneven distribution of capital(s) and power, and are the product of historical struggles. The field operates as '... a set of conditions for the production of cultural practices and the production of producers of these practices. It is not a vague social background but a structured and structuring space...' (Bottrell and France 2015: 103). A detailed consideration of habitus and capitals is incomplete without understanding how the field operates in the lives of young people, such that we believe the concept of field is an essential part of any analysis that aims to grasp how social class inequalities play out in contemporary times.

REFERENCES

Atkinson, W. (2015). *Class*. Cambridge: Polity Press.

Bates, I., Clarke, J., Cohen, P., Finn, D., Moore, R., & Willis, P. (1984). *Schooling for the dole? The new vocationalism.*. London: Macmillan Publishers.

Bottrell, D., & France, A. (2015). Bourdieusian cultural transitions: Young people negotiating 'Fields' in their pathways into and out of crime. In D. Woodman & A. Bennett (Ed.), *Youth cultures, transitions and generations: Bridging the gap in youth research*. London: Palgrave Macmillan.

Bourdieu, P. (1977). *Outline of a theory of practice*. Cambridge: Cambridge University Press.

Bourdieu, P. (1998a). *Acts of resistance: Against the new myths of our time*. Oxford: Polity Press.

Bourdieu, P. (1998b). *Practical reason: On the theory of action*. Stanford: Stanford University Press.

Connell, R. (2007). *Southern theory: The global dynamics of knowledge in social science*. Crows Nest, Australia: Allen and Unwin.

Côté, J. (2014). Towards a new political economy of youth. *Journal of Youth Studies, 14*(4), 527–543.

France, A. (2017). Review Essay: Youth, Social Change and Inequality, Journal of International and Comparative Social Policy.

France, A., & Roberts, S. (2015). The problem of social generations: A critique of the new emerging orthodoxy in youth studies. *Journal of Youth Studies, 18*(2), 215–230.

France, A., & Threadgold, S. (2016). Youth and political economy: Towards a Bourdieusian approach. *Journal of Youth Studies, 19*(5), 612–628.

Moi, T. (1991). Appropriating Bourdieu: feminist theory and Pierre Bourdieu's society of culture. *New Literary History, 22*(4), 1017–1049.

Roberts, K. (1995). *Youth and employment in modern Britain*. Oxford: Oxford University Press.

Roberts, S., & France, A. (2016) The smashed avo debate misses inequality within generations *The Conversation* https://theconversation.com/the-smashed-avo-debate-misses-inequality-within-generations-70475.

Savage, M. (2015). *Social Class in the 21st Century*. London: Pelican.

Savage, M. (2015b). Introduction to elites: From the 'problematic of the proletariat' to a class analysis of 'wealth elites'. *Sociological Review, 63*(2), 223–239.

Threadgold, S. (2015) Bourdieu and the (non) genre of Dolewave (on-line blog) https://youthclassculture.wordpress.com/2015/05/26/bourdieu-and-the-nongenre-of-dolewave/.

Wacquant, L. (2013). Symbolic power and group-making: On Pierre Bourdieu's reframing of class. *Journal of Classical Sociology, 13*(2), 274–291.

Woodman, D., & Wyn, J. (2015). *Youth and generation: Rethinking change and inequality in the lives of young people.* Los Angeles: Sage.

INDEX

A
Aboriginal and Torres Strait Islander, *see* Indigenous
Antipodes, 3, 4, 9, 11, 13, 23, 105, 124, 138, 139
Apprenticeship, 43, 44, 102, 136
Aspiration, 45, 50, 51, 52, 53, 80, 81, 106, 108, 137
Atkinson, Will, 3, 10, 16, 17, 18, 20, 25, 26, 28, 80, 117, 135

B
Beck, Ulrich, 17, 18
Black Capital, 122, 123, 127
Bourdieu, 1–5, 9, 11, 20, 25, 26, 27, 28, 29, 30, 31, 39, 45, 50, 51, 53, 57, 69, 77, 81, 82, 87, 92, 101, 107–109, 113–114, 115, 116, 117–121, 122, 123, 124, 126, 127, 135, 136, 137, 138, 139
Bourdieusian framework, 108, 119, 121, 136, 137

C
Centre for Comtemporary Cultural Studies (CCC), 21–22, 106

Class
  Class Theory, 3, 5, 9, 16, 18, 20, 23, 31, 92
  Death of Class, 22, 31
  History of Class, 4, 19
Classlessness, 13, 137, 138
Classless Societies, 135, 138
Colonialism, 12, 13, 103, 104, 119, 120, 124, 125, 126, 127
Cultural Capital, 15, 25, 28, 29, 52, 58, 74, 82, 85, 89, 114–115, 119, 121–122

D
Devine, Fiona, 3, 17
Doxa, 135, 137–139

E
Economic Capital, 28, 29, 52, 58, 89, 124, 126
Education, 5, 12, 16, 18, 20, 21–22, 23, 24, 25, 28, 30, 39–55, 57–58, 60, 69, 70, 72, 75, 77, 78, 80, 81, 82, 83, 84, 85, 86, 88, 89, 90, 92, 102, 104–105, 108, 114, 115, 117, 120, 121, 122, 123–124, 126, 136, 139

© The Author(s) 2017
A. France, S. Roberts, *Youth and Social Class*,
DOI 10.1057/978-1-137-57829-7

143

Education (*cont.*)
  Fisher Act 1918, 40
  Post-compulsory education, 30, 39–41, 60
  Elite Institutions, 55, 56, 87, 88, 123
  Elite Schools, 53
  Embourgeoisement, 21, 31n1
  Employment, 12, 13, 21, 30, 40, 41, 42, 43, 44, 45, 57–58, 59, 69–89, 92, 102, 104, 105, 109, 116, 137, 139
  Ethnicity, 48, 104, 108, 109, 113, 116, 118, 122, 123

F
Femininity, 107–108, 115, 116
Field, 1, 2, 21, 22, 25, 27, 30, 31, 39, 40, 45, 46, 52, 54, 56, 57, 60, 70, 71, 77–78, 81, 83, 87, 88, 92, 107, 113, 114, 115, 116, 117, 118, 119, 120, 126, 127, 128, 135, 136, 139, 140
  Subfield, 31, 92
France, Alan, 23, 30, 40, 41, 43, 45, 46, 48, 49, 50, 58, 73–75, 78, 82, 102, 103, 104, 105, 106, 108, 125, 135
Furlong, Andy, 23, 54, 73, 74, 76

G
Gender, 3, 5, 55, 102, 105–108, 112–119, 127, 136
Gifting, 90
Grandparent Support, *see* Parental Support
Griffin, Christine, 22, 23, 106, 109, 111

H
Habitus, 25–28, 30, 39, 52, 53, 54, 55, 57, 60, 81, 87, 92, 114, 116–117, 118, 119, 123, 124, 126, 127
Higher Education, 46, 47, 48, 50, 51, 54, 55, 84, 104, 120, 122, 136, 139
  University, 16, 21, 40, 41, 42, 45, 48, 49, 50, 51, 53, 54, 55, 56, 57, 58, 59, 60, 78, 82, 83, 84, 85, 86, 87, 88, 91, 102, 103, 105, 122, 123, 136
Housing, 6, 41, 76, 81, 91, 108, 110

I
Independent Living, 91
Indigenous, 5, 11, 57, 101, 103, 104, 105, 111, 112, 124, 125, 126, 127
  Aboriginal and Torres Strait, 5, 101, 104, 105, 124, 125, 126
  Māori, 12, 13, 101, 104, 105, 111, 124–127
Industrialised Society, 10, 18, 48
Institution Choice, 55
Intergenerational Inequality, 89
Intersectional, 5, 101, 102, 112, 113, 114, 116, 117, 122, 127, 136
Intragenerational Inequality, 119

M
Māori, *see* Indigenous
Marginalisation, 75, 76, 107, 110, 112, 127
Masculinity, 107–109, 115, 117–119
Massification, 39, 46, 48
McRobbie, Angela, 22, 106

INDEX 145

Middle-Class
  Nature of Class, 39, 69
  Underclass, 10, 30, 71, 72
  Upper Class, 10, 107
  Working-class, 9, 13, 21–22, 45, 48, 50–52, 53, 54, 55, 56, 57, 70, 71, 80, 81, 82, 83, 84, 86, 87, 88, 90, 103, 106, 107–110, 114–116, 118, 119, 122–123, 136
Missing Middle, 24

N

NEET (Not in Education, Employment or Training), 72, 86, 138

P

Parental Support, 86
Political Economy, 4, 72, 135
Polytechnic, *see* Post
Postmodernism, 114
Post-structuralism, 17, 107, 110, 111, 127
Post Subcultures, 4
Private Education, 24, 53
Private School, 24, 52, 86
Privilege, 24, 29, 40, 48, 55, 56, 57, 80, 84, 85, 88–91, 113, 120, 122, 125, 139
Public School, 12

R

Race, 5, 11, 12, 57, 102, 103, 104, 109, 110, 111, 112, 113, 115, 116, 117, 119, 120, 121, 122, 123, 124, 127, 136

Reay, Diane, 53, 54, 55, 56, 114, 115, 122, 123
Reflexive, 18, 27, 28, 80
  Pre-reflexive, 27
Research Agenda, 60, 135, 139
Risk Society, 17
Roberts, Ken, 2, 44
Roberts, Steve, 16, 18, 22, 23, 24, 41

S

School Choice, 54, 55
School-to-work transition, 5, 22, 24, 41, 69
Sexuality, 105, 108, 113, 114, 116, 136
Skeggs, Beverley, 3, 18, 31, 53, 76, 113, 114, 115, 116
Social and Economic Status (SES), 3, 12, 13, 45, 48, 49, 50, 51, 52, 57, 80, 82, 91, 102, 103, 104, 125
Social Capital, 24, 26, 28, 29, 30, 56, 82, 85, 86, 89, 119, 123, 127
Social Class, 2–5, 10, 12, 13, 15, 21, 25, 26, 29, 30, 31, 47, 48, 50, 51, 53, 54, 56, 58, 60, 69, 70, 71, 76, 77, 79, 84, 86, 87, 89, 101, 102, 114, 122, 123, 135, 137, 139
Social Construction, 25, 40
Social Generation, 19, 23, 73
Social Networks, 29, 81, 87, 115, 123
Social Order, 29, 137
Social Reproduction, 3, 5, 21, 22, 23, 31, 39, 45, 47, 60, 83, 92, 102, 106, 136, 139
Social Space, 2, 25, 26, 29, 30, 80, 115, 126
Struggle, 17, 25, 30, 47, 52, 56, 59, 60, 83, 88, 90, 128, 135, 139
Student Employment, 58, 78

Symbolic Economy, 54, 119
Symbolic Violence, 29, 114

T
Thatcher, Jenny, 3, 71

U
Underemployment, 44, 69, 82, 92, 105, 137
Unemployment, 41, 43, 69, 70, 71, 72, 75, 78, 80, 81, 82, 105
University, *see* Higher Education
Upskill, 44, 47

V
Vocational
Post, 12, 17, 46, 60, 73, 79, 89, 92, 107, 110, 111, 114, 117, 119, 127, 136

TAFE, 43, 45, 83
VET, 44, 45, 49, 83, 102, 116

W
Wacquant, Loic, 26, 29, 30, 78, 120, 139
Welfare, 12, 59, 71, 72
Willis, Paul, 22, 54, 70, 103, 106
Woodman, Dan, 19, 23, 73, 76, 77, 136
Wyn, Johanna, 23, 73, 77, 83, 136

Y
Youth-as-class, 73

Z
Zombie Category, 1, 18, 19, 31

Printed by Printforce, the Netherlands